Briefly: Aquinas'
Summa Theologica
(God, Part I)

David Mills Daniel

scm press

© David Mills Daniel 2006

The Author has asserted his right under the Copyright, Designs and
Patents Act, 1988, to be identified as the Author of this Work

The author and publisher acknowledge material reproduced from
Basic Writings of Saint Thomas Aquinas, vol. I,
ed. A. C. Pegis, 1997, Indianapolis/Cambridge: Hackett Publishing
Company, ISBN 0872203898. Reprinted by permission of
Hackett Publishing Company, Inc. All rights reserved.

British Library Cataloguing in Publication data

A catalogue record for this book is available
from the British Library

0 334 04035 3/978 0 334 04035 4

First published in 2006 by SCM Press
9–17 St Alban's Place,
London N1 0NX

www.scm-canterburypress.co.uk

SCM Press is a division of
SCM-Canterbury Press Ltd

Printed and bound in Great Britain by
Bookmarque Ltd, Croydon, Surrey

Contents

Introduction   ix

Context   I

Who was Thomas Aquinas?   I
What is the *Summa Theologica*?   2
Some Issues to Consider   II
Suggestions for Further Reading   13

Detailed Summary of Thomas Aquinas'
Summa Theologica   14

God (Part I)

Question I   The Nature and Domain of Sacred
    Doctrine

First Article   Whether, Besides the Philosophical
    Disciplines, Any Further Doctrine Is Required?   14

Question II   The Existence of God

First Article   Whether the Existence of God Is
    Self-Evident?   15
Second Article   Whether It Can Be Demonstrated
    that God Exists?   17
Third Article   Whether God Exists?   18

Contents

Question III   On the Simplicity of God
First Article   Whether God Has a Body?   21

Question IV   The Perfection of God
First Article   Whether God Is Perfect?   23

Question VI   The Goodness of God
First Article   Whether to Be Good Belongs to God?   24
Second Article   Whether God Is the Highest Good?   25
Fourth Article   Whether all Things Are Good
   by the Divine Goodness?   26

Question VII   The Infinity of God
First Article   Whether God Is Infinite?   27

Question IX   The Immutability of God
First Article Whether God Is Altogether Immutable?   28

Question X   The Eternity of God
Second Article   Whether God Is Eternal?   29

Question XII   How God Is Known by Us
First Article   Whether Any Created Intellect Can
   See the Essence of God?   30
Twelfth Article   Whether God Can Be Known
   in this Life by Natural Reason?   32
Thirteenth Article   Whether by Grace a Higher
   Knowledge of God Can Be Obtained than by
   Natural Reason?   33

Question XIII   The Names of God
First Article   Whether a Name Can Be Given to God?   34

Contents

Second Article   Whether Any Name Can Be Applied
to God Substantially?   35
Third Article   Whether Any Name Can Be Applied
to God Properly?   37
Fourth Article   Whether Names Applied to God
Are Synonymous?   39
Fifth Article   Whether what Is Said of God and
of Creatures Is Univocally Predicated of Them?   40
Sixth Article   Whether Names Predicated of God
Are Predicated Primarily of Creatures?   42
Twelfth Article   Whether Affirmative Propositions
Can Be Formed About God?   43

Question XXV   The Power of God

Second Article   Whether the Power of God Is
Infinite?   44
Third Article   Whether God Is Omnipotent?   45
Fifth Article   Whether God Can Do what He
Does not?   48

Overview   50

Glossary   77

Introduction

The SCM *Briefly* series is designed to enable students and general readers to acquire knowledge and understanding of key texts in philosophy, philosophy of religion, theology and ethics. While the series will be especially helpful to those following university and A-level courses in philosophy, ethics and religious studies, it will in fact be of interest to anyone looking for a short guide to the ideas of a particular philosopher or theologian.

Each book in the series takes a piece of work by one philosopher and provides a summary of the original text, which adheres closely to it, and contains direct quotations from it, thus enabling the reader to follow each development in the philosopher's argument(s). Throughout the summary, there are page references to the original philosophical writing, so that the reader has ready access to the primary text. In the Introduction to each book, you will find details of the edition of the philosophical work referred to.

In *Briefly: Aquinas' Summa Theologica*, we refer to *Basic Writings of Saint Thomas Aquinas*, vol. I, edited by Anton C. Pegis, 1997, Indianapolis/Cambridge: Hackett Publishing Company, ISBN 0872203898.

Each *Briefly* begins with an Introduction, followed by a chapter on the Context in which the work was written. Who was this writer? Why was this book written? With Some

Introduction

Issues to Consider, and some Suggested Further Reading, this *Briefly* aims to get anyone started in their philosophical investigation. The detailed summary of the philosophical work is followed by a concise chapter-by-chapter overview and an extensive glossary of terms.

Bold type is used in the Detailed Summary and Overview sections to indicate the first occurence of words and phrases that appear in the Glossary. The Glossary also contains terms used elsewhere in this *Briefly* guide and other terms that readers may encounter in their study of Aquinas' *Summa Theologica*.

Context

Who was Thomas Aquinas?

Thomas Aquinas, the son of Landulf, Count of Aquino, was born at the castle of Roccasecca, near Naples, in 1224 or 1225, and educated at the Benedictine Abbey of Monte Cassino and the University of Naples. While a student, he decided to enter the order of Dominican friars. This was against the wishes of his parents, who wanted him to become a Benedictine monk. Despite being kidnapped and held prisoner by his family, Aquinas refused to change his mind and, after his release, the Dominicans sent him to the University of Paris in 1245. There he became a student of Albert the Great, the Dominican philosopher and theologian, going with him to the University of Cologne in 1248. Aquinas returned to Paris in 1252, eventually becoming Dominican professor of theology there. He moved to Rome in 1259, where, because of his growing reputation as philosopher, theologian and reconciler of Aristotelian philosophy with Christian teaching, he became adviser to a succession of popes, while continuing to teach (in Rome, Bologna, Paris and Naples) and to write prolifically. In 1274, when he was travelling from Naples to take part in the Second Council of Lyons, he died at the monastery of Fossanuova, near Rome. He was canonized in 1323 and, in 1879, Pope Leo XIII declared that his setting forth of Roman Catholic teaching was definitive. His books include *De Ente et Essentia* (1254–6), the *Summa Contra Gentiles* (1258–64), the *De Veritate* (1256–9) and the *Summa Theologica* (*Summa Theologiae*, 1265–72).

What is the *Summa Theologica*?

In the introduction to his edition of the *Summa Theologica*, A. C. Pegis describes it as a 'truly monumental synthesis and exposition of Christian thought'; and even after more than 700 years, it remains an essential resource for any student of the philosophy of religion or Christian theology. But the *Summa Theologica* is 'monumental' in length (the first volume of the Pegis edition is almost 1,000 pages), as well as in the quality of its content, so this *Briefly* (God, Part I) covers only some sections of the first volume. These include Aquinas' arguments for the existence of God (the five ways), some of God's attributes, how human beings can have knowledge of God and how it is possible to talk about God. Future *Brieflys* will cover other sections from the Pegis edition.

The nature and role of sacred doctrine (Question I)

Aquinas deals with the issue of why revelation is necessary, when human beings can learn about God by using their reason. As they are capable of investigating such fundamental questions as 'Does God exist?' and 'Is God good?' through philosophical enquiry, why do they need to bother with sacred doctrine?

His answer is that, although there are some religious truths (such as God's existence and goodness), which can be discovered by reason, others (such as the Trinity: that God is three in one) are beyond human reason. Therefore, revelation is needed. But even those religious truths that can be known through reason can be also be known through revelation, and believed on the basis of faith, rather than rational argument. If there were some religious truths that could only be discovered through reason, they would not be available to those who cannot understand philosophical arguments.

Another important point here is that, although Aquinas was a Dominican friar, who believed in God through faith, and had dedicated his life to God's service, he valued philosophical enquiry. Medieval theologians like Aquinas did not see revelation and reason as mutually exclusive sources of knowledge about God, with those who accepted God's revelation in faith discarding reason. They believed that human beings are made in God's image, with a God-given intellect that should be used in God's service. In addition to being a means of discovering some religious truths, reason also has an important role to play in exploring and understanding what God has revealed. Theology is, after all, an intellectual activity.

God's existence (Question II)

Can God's existence be proved by natural reason? Aquinas believes that it can, but not by an *a priori* argument from the concept of God to his existence. He has in mind what has come to be known as the ontological argument, put forward by St Anselm in his *Proslogion*. Aquinas does not accept that once the term 'God' is understood, it is seen that the proposition 'God exists' is self-evident. He distinguishes between things that are self-evident in themselves and also to us, and things that are self-evident in themselves but not to us. In a self-evident proposition, the predicate is included in the essence of the subject, as in 'Man is an animal', so if we know the essence of both predicate and subject, the proposition will be self-evident. However, if we do not, the proposition will be self-evident in itself, but not to us. 'God exists' is not self-evident because, as God is his own existence, subject and predicate are the same, and, as we do not know God's essence, the proposition is not self-evident to us. For Aquinas, if we knew God's essence, we would know that God is a being that must exist. However, we do not know his essence, so his existence is not self-evident.

So how can we prove God's existence? Aquinas explains that there are two kinds of proof: those that start with God and those that start with God's effects. As God's creatures, with all the limitations of finite existence, human beings do not have access to God's essence, so we cannot start from God. However, we do have access to God's effects: the world he has made and all it contains. Therefore, we need to use *a posteriori* arguments, which start with experience. This is why Aquinas' type of argument is known as a cosmological argument: it begins with the world, and our experience of it, and argues from the world to God. Of course, to be thinking about the world in relation to God is to be experiencing it as something that requires an explanation beyond itself. Only those who wonder why there is a world, or why it is the kind of world it is, will experience it in this way.

But can such an argument give us knowledge of God? Aquinas concedes that it will not provide perfect knowledge of God, because effects (the finite world) and cause (infinite God) are not in proportion. But, as every effect depends upon its cause, if there is an effect, there must be a cause, so the existence of the cause (God) can be proved. Aquinas puts forward five proofs, known as the 'five ways'. It is not clear whether he intended they should always be taken together, or thought they could stand alone. They all move from the world, or features of it (Aquinas' fifth way is a teleological argument), to God's existence (see the Detailed Summary and Overview sections for the five ways). Aquinas considers that the arguments he puts forward show the inadequacy of a non-theistic account of the world: that natural things can be explained by nature and human decisions by human reason. Both what happens in nature and what happens as a result of human reason must be traced back to a higher cause, a self-necessary first principle: God.

The third way, which makes a clear distinction between finite or contingent things (those, like the world and all it contains, which are things that can not-be) and an infinite, necessary being (God, on which contingent things depend), is regarded by Thomists as the most important one. In his book, *Aquinas*, Father Frederick Copleston, identifies the third way as 'fundamental', because it contains the main idea of *a posteriori* arguments for the existence of God: the 'dependence' of the world on God. If 'the existence of finite being' (the world) is seen as a problem, the only answer is to affirm the existence of a necessary and infinite being: God.

But is the cosmological argument any more convincing to the atheist or sceptic than the ontological argument that Aquinas rejects? In his *Dialogues Concerning Natural Religion* (Part IX), David Hume provides a detailed refutation of it. First, he does not accept it is an *a posteriori* argument. It is an *a priori* one, because it is not based on experience (except to the extent that there is a world), but on a certain view of the world: that it is contingent (one that can not-be) and that its existence can only be explained if there is something that has necessary existence: God. As it involves necessary existence, it is vulnerable to the same kind of criticisms as the ontological argument. It may be claimed (Hume argues) that God is a necessarily existent being, and that if we knew his 'whole essence or nature', we would see that it is impossible for him not to exist; but, given our limited faculties, we are not going to. As things stand, God, like every other being, can be thought of as non-existent, because no contradiction is involved. Therefore, the words ' "necessary existence" have no meaning'.

But (Hume continues), if we require something to be necessarily existent, why should it not be the material universe itself, rather than God? The universe may contain qualities which, if we knew about them, would make its non-existence seem as great a contradiction as twice two being five. And if it is argued that the world (and everything in it) is contingent, and can be thought of as being destroyed or altered, the same is true of God. We can think of him as not existing, or his attributes as altered. Again, in a succession of objects, each one is caused by the one that precedes it. To state the chain of causes is to provide a full explanation of how each individual object came into existence. It is pointless and absurd, having heard such an explanation, to ask what is the single cause of the succession of objects (that is, all the things in the universe) as a whole.

As an objective proof of God's existence, the cosmological argument does not work. Some people simply do not wonder why there is a universe, nor do they see it as contingent and finite. Like Bertrand Russell, they think it just exists, and does not need a necessary and infinite being to explain its existence. So does the cosmological argument have any value? Copleston indicates the level at which it may work, when he talks about seeing the existence of finite being as a problem.

The cosmological argument may help those people who do wonder why there is a universe, and who do see it as contingent and requiring an explanation in terms of something beyond itself, to relate their perception of the nature of the world to its creator and cause.

God's attributes

Goodness (Question VI)

Aquinas touches on another major issue in his discussion of God's existence: the problem of evil. If God is infinitely good, why is there evil in the world? His answer is that God is the highest good, and would not allow evil in the world unless, through his omnipotence and infinite goodness, he could bring good out of it. Indeed, being good belongs pre-eminently to God, as he is the highest good, and all perfections in created things come from him as the first cause. However, unlike a univocal cause, which is uniformly like its effects, God is an equivocal cause, and so is unlike his effects.

Power (Question XXV)

God is infinitely powerful or omnipotent, but this raises issues. What does it mean to say that God is all-powerful? Are there no limits to God's power? Aquinas explains that God can do all possible things, and that there are two ways in which something is possible. The first is in relation to the powers of created beings, such as human beings, whose powers are limited. So, for example, it is possible for human beings to run, but not at 100 miles an hour. However, God's powers are not limited in any way. But although he is able to do all things that are possible absolutely, something involving a contradiction (which is the case when subject and predicate are incompatible, as in the statement, 'that man is an ass') is not possible absolutely, and so cannot fall within God's omnipotence. This is not because God's power is defective, but because it is not possible.

But can God do what he does not do? Aquinas points out a common mistake, which is to think that God acts from natural necessity, so that nothing can happen except what actually does. However, God causes all things, so there is no necessity in the present order of creation that rules out things being other than they are. God's wisdom established the present order of creation, but is not limited to it. God could have produced a different one, and he can do other things than those he has done.

Eternity (Question X)

This is a difficult concept for the human intellect to grasp, given that we are finite beings. Aquinas warns that it is all too easy for us to think our ways of trying to understand eternity reflect its reality: for example, our idea of eternity being the now standing still. Again, language can be misleading. We say God is before and after eternity, but this is just a way of saying he endures beyond every kind of given duration. We also talk of eternity as if it is a kind of measure, but this is to do with our limited understanding of it, and does not mean that God is measured.

Other attributes (Questions III, IV, VII and IX)

For Aquinas' discussion of God's simplicity (Question III), perfection (Question IV), infinity (Question VII) and immutability (Question IX), see the Detailed Summary and Overview sections.

How we know about God (Question XII)

God is infinite, and there is an infinite distance between the created intellects of human beings and God: so will we ultimately be able to see God's essence? Aquinas rejects the view that no created intellect can ever see God's essence, because it would mean human beings could not attain beatitude. Therefore, it must be possible for us to reach the first cause of things and see God's essence; and this is supported by Christian teachings that refer to the vision of understanding. Further, human beings have a relationship to God: that of effects to their cause; and this is how created intellects can be proportioned to know God.

But can we know about God in this life by natural reason? As natural knowledge starts with the senses, it can extend only to things that can be known through the senses, and the senses cannot enable our intellects to see God's essence in this life. However, although we cannot know God's whole power from sensible things, this does not mean we cannot obtain any knowledge of him in this life. Sensible things depend on God as their cause, and from them we can at least know that God exists; and that he is the first cause of all things, who is much greater than, and completely different from, everything he causes.

Will grace give us a greater knowledge of God than natural reason? In the acquisition of knowledge, our reason is helped by the light of grace. Further, although grace does not make it possible to know what God is in this life, there are some religious truths, such as God being three in one, which can only be known through revelation.

Talking about God (Question XIII)

As God is infinite and omnipotent, and created everything from nothing, while human beings are finite and created, how is it possible for us to talk about God? As God's essence is beyond anything human beings can understand and express in words, any language we use about God is going to be inadequate; it is not going to capture his full reality. However, Aquinas explains that, although we cannot see God's essence in this world, we do know something about him from creatures, as he has caused them. Thus, we can base the language we use about God on creatures.

But, given the distance between human beings and God, is it the case that, when we make positive statements about God, we are actually saying what he is not? Aquinas acknowledges some people think that such terms as 'good' or 'wise', although they appear to be applied affirmatively to God, express what he is not, rather than what he is, so to say that God 'lives' just indicates he is not like inanimate things; and that others think the terms used of God refer to his relationship with creatures, so to say God is 'good' means he causes goodness in things. But he does not accept either view. If saying God is 'good' means he causes good things, then all the terms applied to God are being used in a secondary sense, and this is not what people think they are doing when they speak of God. The terms do signify the divine substance, but they only represent God as far as our intellects know him.

However, when terms are used to refer to both God and creatures, are they being used univocally (with the same meaning) or equivocally (with a different meaning)? Aquinas explains that they are not being used univocally, because of the difference between God and his creatures: the effects (creatures) fall short of their cause (God). The perfections found in creatures are divided and multiplied but, in God, they pre-exist unitedly. So, when the term 'wise' is applied to a human being, it comprehends the thing it indicates, but it does not do so in relation to God, because God exceeds what the term signifies. But the terms are not used equivocally either because, if they were, nothing could be known or proved about God on the basis of his creatures. The terms are used of God and creatures analogously, which means that what is said of God and creatures is on the basis that creatures are related to God as their cause. With analogous use of terms, the idea is not one and the same (as when something is said univocally), nor is it totally different (as when it is said equivocally). So, when we talk about God, we must distinguish between the attributes or perfections being referred to and the language we are using to express them. Use of such terms as 'good' and 'wise' about God signifies that these perfections exist more excellently in God than creatures, and apply primarily to him, because they flow from him to creatures. However, the terms themselves are applied primarily to creatures, because we know creatures first.

Some Issues to Consider

- Aquinas believed that revelation was necessary, because there are some religious truths that cannot be discovered by reason, and if there were religious truths that could only be known through reason, they would not be available to those who cannot understand philosophical arguments.
- Aquinas rejected the ontological argument for God's existence, holding that God's existence can only be proved by an *a posteriori* argument that begins with our experience of the world, and argues from the world to God.

- Thomists tend to regard Aquinas' third way, which draws a clear distinction between finite or contingent things (the world and everything in it) and an infinite necessary being (God), as the most important of his fives ways of proving God's existence.
- Is David Hume's refutation of the cosmological argument convincing?
- Is the world finite, contingent and dependent, and does it require an explanation in terms of something beyond itself?
- Is it satisfactory to say that God would not allow evil in the world unless, through his omnipotence and infinite goodness, he could bring good out of it; and is there evidence he is doing so?
- Aquinas explains that God's omnipotence means that he can do all things that are possible absolutely, but something involving a contradiction is not possible absolutely, and so cannot fall within God's omnipotence.
- The eternity of God is a difficult concept for human beings to grasp, and it is all too easy for us to think that our ways of trying to understand it reflect its reality.
- Aquinas rejects the view that no created intellect can ever see God's essence, because it would mean human beings could not attain beatitude.
- Our senses cannot enable our intellects to see God's essence in this life but, as sensible things depend on God as their cause, we can learn from them that God exists.
- Any language we use about God is going to be inadequate but, as we know something about God from his creatures, we can base the language we use about God on creatures.
- When we talk about God, what the terms we use refer to, such as goodness and life, belong primarily to God, not creatures, but the way they are expressed is based on creatures, and does not apply properly to God.

- When terms are used of both God and creatures, they are used analogously, which means what is said of God and creatures is on the basis that creatures are related to God as their cause. When terms are used in this way, the idea is not one and the same, nor is it totally different.
- When such terms as 'good' and 'wise' are used of God, they signify these perfections exist more excellently in God than creatures, and apply primarily to him, because they flow from him to creatures; but the terms themselves are applied primarily to creatures, because creatures are known first.

Suggestions for Further Reading

Basic Writings of Saint Thomas Aquinas, vol. I, ed. A. C. Pegis, 1997, Indianapolis/Cambridge: Hackett Publishing Company (contains the *Summa Theologica*, Part I).

Basic Writings of Saint Thomas Aquinas, vol. II, ed. A. C. Pegis, 1997, Indianapolis/Cambridge: Hackett Publishing Company.

Anselm, Proslogion with the Replies of Gaunilo and Anselm, ed. T. Williams, 2001, Indianapolis/Cambridge: Hackett Publishing Company.

F. C. Copleston, 1955, *Aquinas*, Harmondsworth: Penguin.

A. Nichols, 2002, *Discovering Aquinas: An introduction to his life, work and influence*, London: Darton, Longman and Todd.

J. H. Hick, 1990, *Philosophy of Religion*, fourth edition, Englewood Cliffs, New Jersey: Prentice Hall.

R. Swinburne, 1991, *The Existence of God*, revised edition, Oxford: Clarendon Press.

P. Vardy, 1999, *The Puzzle of God*, revised edition, London: Fount Paperbacks.

Detailed Summary of Thomas Aquinas' *Summa Theologica*

God (Part I)

Question I The Nature and Domain of Sacred Doctrine

First Article Whether, Besides the Philosophical Disciplines, Any Further Doctrine Is Required? (pp. 5–6)

Objection 1 As human beings should not seek knowledge that is 'above reason', we seem to need only the '**philosophical disciplines**' (p. 5). Any other **doctrine** is 'superfluous' (p. 5).

Obj. 2 Doctrine can concern only being, for only the true, 'which is convertible with being', can be known (p. 5). Even God is considered in **philosophy**, of which, 'as is clear from **Aristotle**', **theology** is a branch (p. 5).

On the contrary, God-inspired **scripture** is not part of philosophy, which is 'discovered by **human reason**' (p. 5).

I answer that, in addition to philosophy, 'a doctrine revealed by God' was needed, as this is the only way that truths that 'exceed human reason' can be made known (p. 6). For the truths about God that can be known through reason would be available only to a few, would take a long time to discover, and would contain 'many errors' (p. 6). Thus, '**sacred doctrine** by way of revelation' was necessary to ensure our '**salvation**' (p. 6).

Reply Obj. 1   What is beyond human beings' knowledge cannot be sought through reason, but what **God** reveals must be 'accepted through **faith**'; and these are the things of which 'sacred doctrine consists' (p. 6).

Reply Obj. 2   Different sciences can establish the same truths in different ways (p. 6). So, there is no reason why matters which are dealt with in philosophy, as 'known by the light' of human reason, should not also by dealt with as 'known by the light of the divine revelation' (p. 6). Thus, the theology that is part of sacred doctrine 'differs in **genus**' from that which belongs to philosophy (p. 6).

Question II   The Existence of God

First Article   Whether the Existence of God Is Self-Evident? *(pp. 18–20)*

Objection 1   The **existence of God** seems '**self-evident**', because it 'exists naturally in us' (p. 18).

Obj. 2   Things are said to be self-evident if 'known as soon as the terms are known' (p. 18). Once the nature of a whole and a part are known, it is immediately seen that 'every whole is greater than its part' (p. 18). And, once the 'name *God*' is understood, it is seen that God must exist, as God is that '**than which nothing greater can be conceived**' (pp. 18–19). To exist '**actually**' is greater that to exist 'only **mentally**', so, if the 'name *God*' exists mentally, it follows it 'exists actually' (p. 19). Thus, the **proposition** '*God exists* is self-evident' (p. 19).

Obj. 3   The existence of truth is self-evident. But, 'God is truth itself', so God's existence 'is self-evident' (p. 19).

On the contrary, it is impossible to 'mentally admit the opposite of what is self-evident' (p. 19). However, the opposite of the proposition '*God is* can be mentally admitted' (p. 19). So, 'God exists is not self-evident' (p. 19).

I answer that, there are 'two ways' in which something can be self-evident: in itself and not to us, and in itself and to us (p. 19). A **self-evident proposition** is one where 'the **predicate** is included in the **essence** of the **subject**': for example, '*Man is an animal*' (p. 19). If the essence of both predicate and subject is known, the proposition will be self-evident; but, if it is not, 'the proposition will be self-evident in itself, but not to those who do not know the meaning of the predicate and subject of the proposition' (p. 19). Thus, '*God exists*' is not a self-evident proposition, because, as 'God is His own existence', subject and predicate are the same (p. 19). And, not knowing 'the essence of God', the proposition is not self-evident to us, but needs to be '**demonstrated** by things that are more known to us': 'His **effects**' (p. 19).

Reply Obj. 1   A 'general and confused' knowledge of God's existence is '**implanted in us by nature**', although this is not **absolute knowledge** of God's existence, just as knowing someone is approaching is not the same as knowing 'Peter is approaching', even though it is Peter (p. 19).

Reply Obj. 2   Not everyone may understand the 'name *God*' to 'signify something than which nothing greater can be thought' (p. 20). And, even if everyone did, he might not understand that it signified something that actually exists, as opposed to something existing 'mentally' (p. 20). It cannot be argued that it exists actually, unless 'it be admitted that there actually exists something than which nothing greater can be thought': which is precisely what those who deny God's existence do not admit (p. 20).

Reply Obj. 3   The existence of 'truth in general' is self-evident to us, but not that of 'a **Primal Truth**' (p. 20).

The Existence of God

Second Article Whether It Can Be Demonstrated that God Exists? (pp. 20–1)

Objection 1 It seems that God's existence cannot be demonstrated, as it is an '**article of faith** that God exists' (p. 20). And things of faith, which are 'of the unseen', cannot be demonstrated, because that produces '**scientific knowledge**' (p. 20).

Obj. 2 Essence is the '**middle term** of demonstration', but we cannot know 'in what God's essence consists', only in what it does not (p. 20).

Obj. 3 Further, if God's existence is to be demonstrated, this would be 'from his effects' (p. 20). However, his effects are '**finite**', whereas he is '**infinite**' (p. 20). As a **cause** cannot be demonstrated by an effect not 'proportioned to it', God's existence cannot be demonstrated (p. 20).

On the contrary, in Romans 1.20, **St Paul** writes that the '*invisible things*' **of God** are understood through those which are made (p. 20). But this would not be so, unless God's existence could by demonstrated, because the 'first thing' we must know about anything is whether it exists (p. 20).

I answer that, there are two kinds of demonstration. One is 'through the cause', and the other 'through the effect' (p. 20). When we know an effect better than its cause, we move from the effect to 'knowledge of the cause' (p. 21). And, as every effect depends upon its cause, if the effect exists, 'the cause must **pre-exist**' it (p. 21). God's existence is 'not self-evident to us', but it can be demonstrated from those of his effects 'which are known to us' (p. 21).

Reply Obj. 1 God's existence, which can be known by '**natural reason**', is not an article of faith, but a **preamble** to it (p. 21). For faith 'presupposes **natural knowledge**' (p. 21). However, those who cannot understand a **proof** can accept, as a matter of faith, something which can be demonstrated.

Reply Obj. 2   When a cause is demonstrated from an effect, it takes the place of the cause's definition 'in proving the cause's existence'(p. 21). This is particularly so with God, because, to prove the existence of anything, the 'meaning of the name', not its essence, must be accepted as a middle term, because essence follows existence (p. 21). God's names derive from his effects, so, in demonstrating God's existence, we 'may take for the middle term the meaning of the name *God*' (p. 21).

Reply Obj. 3   No '**perfect knowledge**' can be obtained from 'effects not proportioned to the cause', but the existence of the cause can be demonstrated from its effects (p. 21). This is so with God, but we cannot know him 'perfectly as He is in His essence' (p. 21).

Third Article   Whether God Exists? (pp. 21–4)

Objection 1   It seems God does not exist, because if 'one of two contraries' is infinite, the other would be destroyed (p. 21). Again, the name 'God', means he 'is **infinite goodness**', but **evil** exists in the world (p. 21).

Obj. 2   It is 'superfluous' to hold that what can be 'accounted for by a few principles' has been 'produced by many' (p. 21). It appears that other principles can account for what we see in the world, even if God does not exist. Natural things can be 'reduced to one principle', nature, and all '**voluntary things**' to 'human reason, or will' (pp. 21–2).

On the contrary, it is said of God (Exodus 3.14): '*I am Who am*' (p. 22).

I answer that, God's existence can be proved 'in **five ways**' (p. 22).

The 'first' way is the argument from motion (p. 22). Evidently, some things in the world 'are in motion', and what moves is moved by something else, because 'motion is nothing else than the reduction of something from **potentiality** to **actuality**' (p. 22). But this can only be done by 'something in a state of actuality', as when fire, which is 'actually hot', makes wood, which is potentially so, actually hot (p. 22). The same thing could not be 'at once in actuality and potentiality in the same respect'; only in different respects (p. 22). For example, what is actually hot could not be potentially so at the same time, although it is also 'potentially cold' (p. 22). Nothing could be '**mover and moved**' at the same time: nothing can move itself (p. 22). Whatever is moved must be moved by something else, and, if the mover is moved, it is moved by something else, and so on. But this cannot continue 'to infinity', because there would then be no first, or any other, mover (p. 22). Thus, there must be a 'first mover, moved by no other', and this is God (p. 22).

The 'second way' is 'from the nature of **efficient cause**' (p. 22). There is 'an order of efficient causes' in the world, and nothing is 'the efficient cause of itself' because, to be so, it would have to be '**prior to itself**' (p. 22). But it is impossible for efficient causes to go on to infinity, because (however many **intermediate causes** there are) the **first cause** causes the intermediate one, and that the '**ultimate cause**' (p. 22). If we remove the cause, we remove the effect so, without a first cause, there will be no other causes. But if we proceed to infinity, there will be no 'first efficient cause', and no intermediate or ultimate effects (p. 22). Therefore, it is 'necessary to admit a first efficient cause', which is God (p. 22).

The 'third way' is from '**possibility and necessity**' (p. 22). In nature, there are things, which, as they are '**generated**' and '**corrupted**', are possible 'to be and not to be' (pp. 22–3). But these things could not always have existed, because 'that which can not-be at some time is not' (p. 23). And, if every-thing is of this kind, there was a time when nothing existed. But, if this were the case, even now nothing would exist, be-cause nothing would have 'begun to exist'; but this is 'absurd' (p. 23). So, not all things are 'merely possible'; there must exist **something that has 'necessary' existence** (p. 23). But the neces-sity of 'every **necessary** thing' is either caused by something else or it is not (p. 23). However, as with 'efficient causes', it is impossible to go 'to infinity' with necessary things, whose necessity is caused by something else (p. 23). So, there must be something 'having of itself its own necessity' (p. 23). And this is God.

The 'fourth way' is from 'the **gradation' of things**; some are more or less good, and so on (p. 23). But *'more* and *less'* are 'predicated of different things', according to the degree to which they resemble a **'maximum'**, such as 'hottest' (p. 23). Thus, there are the 'truest', the 'best', the 'noblest'; and 'some-thing which is most being', as the things that are the 'greatest in truth are greatest in being' (p. 23). The maximum in 'any genus' is the cause of all that belongs to it, as fire, 'the maxi-mum of heat', causes all hot things (p. 23). And so, there must be something, which, in relation to all beings, causes 'their being, goodness, and every other **perfection'** (p. 23).

The 'fifth way' is from 'the **governance of the world'** (p. 23). Things such as '**natural bodies'**, which lack knowledge, none-theless 'act for an end', so as 'to obtain the best result' (p. 23). It is clear they do this **'designedly'** (p. 23). But, as they lack knowledge, they must be 'directed' towards their end by some **intelligent being**, just as an arrow is 'by the archer' (p. 23). Thus, there must be an 'intelligent being', directing natural things to their end; and this is God (p. 23).

Reply Obj. 1 **Augustine** has said that, as God is the *'highest good'*, he would not allow evil in his **creation**, unless, through his **omnipotence** and infinite goodness, he could bring good out of evil (p. 23).

Reply Obj. 2 As nature works for a **'determinate end'** under a **higher agent**'s direction, whatever happens in nature must be traced back to God as 'its first cause' (pp. 23–4). Similarly, what is done 'voluntarily' must be traced back to a higher cause than 'human reason and will', because these can fail (p. 24). **Changeable things**, which can develop **defects**, must be traced back to 'an **immovable** and **self-necessary first principle**' (p. 24).

Question III   On the Simplicity of God

First Article   Whether God Has a Body? (pp. 25–7)

Objection 1   It seems God has a **body**, as '**Holy Scripture**' refers to his having 'three dimensions', as in Job 11.8–9, where he is said to be *'higher than heaven'* and *'deeper than hell'* (p. 25).

Obj. 2   God seems to have a figure, because Genesis 1.26 refers to man being made in his *'image'*.

Obj. 3   Scripture also attributes '**corporeal parts**' to God (p. 26). Psalm 33.16, for example, speaks of God's eyes being open upon the **just**.

Obj. 4   Isaiah 3.13 suggests that God has 'posture', by referring to him as sitting (p. 26).

Obj. 5   Only bodies can be a '**local terminus**', and in Psalm 33.6, it is stated that people should come to God to be enlightened (p. 26).

On the contrary, John 4.24 states that God is a '**spirit**'.

I answer that, there are three ways of showing that God is not a body. A body only moves if it is moved, but God is the '**First Mover**, Himself unmoved' (p. 26). The 'first being' must 'of necessity' be in act, not potentiality (p. 26). Although, when a particular thing passes from potentiality to actuality, 'the potentiality is prior in time to the actuality', actuality is nonetheless prior, because what is potential is 'reduced to actuality only by some being in actuality' (p. 26). Now God is the '**First Being**', and so it is impossible that God should have any potentiality, or be a body (p. 26). Again, God is the 'most noble of beings' (p. 26). However, a body cannot be, because an **animate** body is nobler than an **inanimate** one, but the former is not animate as a body, 'otherwise all bodies would be animate'; it is animated by something else, as our bodies are by the **soul** (p. 26). Animate bodies are 'nobler' than inanimate ones, so God cannot be a body (p. 26).

Reply Obj. 1   Holy Scripture presents **spiritual beings** under the likeness of 'corporeal things', because height, for example, indicates God's **transcendence**; length, the 'duration of His existence'; and so on (pp. 26–7).

Reply Obj. 2   It is not man's body that is made in God's image, but his 'reason and **intellect**' (p. 27).

Reply Obj. 3   Bodily parts are attributed to God in scripture as a convenient way of referring, and drawing attention, to his actions. For example, when it is said that God has an eye, it signifies 'seeing intellectually, not sensibly' (p. 27).

Reply Obj. 4   Similarly with posture: he is said to sit, to indicate his 'unchangeableness and **dominion**' (p. 27).

Reply Obj. 5   When we say that we draw near to God, this signifies 'spiritual affection under the likeness of local motion' (p. 27).

Question IV   The Perfection of God

First Article   Whether God Is Perfect? (pp. 37–8)

Objection 1   God seems not to be perfect, because a thing is said to be perfect, 'if it is completely made' (p. 37). But God is not made.

Obj. 2   God is the 'first beginning of things', but the beginning of anything (such as a seed) seems 'imperfect' (p. 37).

Obj. 3   God's essence is 'being itself', but being seems imperfect, as it is the 'most universal and receptive of all modification' (p. 37).

On the contrary, in Matthew 5:48, we are told to be perfect as 'our heavenly Father' is (p. 37).

I answer that, some '**ancient philosophers**' did not 'predicate *best* and *most perfect* of the first principle', because they thought only in terms of a 'material principle' (p. 37). A material first principle would be very imperfect, because it would be 'absolutely potential' (p. 37). God, on the other hand, is not material, but is the 'most actual' and 'perfect' first principle (p. 37).

Reply Obj. 1   Things that 'come to be' are called 'perfect', when brought 'from potentiality into actuality'; and the term 'signifies by extension whatever is not wanting in actual being' (p. 38).

Reply Obj. 2   The imperfect material principle 'cannot be absolutely first, but is preceded by something perfect' (p. 38). Although a plant comes from a seed, the seed, in its turn, came from a plant (p. 38). Something actual must precede something potential, 'since a potential being can be reduced to act only by some being already actual' (p. 38).

Reply Obj. 3   Being is 'the most perfect of all things', because 'nothing has actuality except so far as it is'; so 'being is the actuality of all things' (p. 38). The 'being' in the 'being of a man' or of a horse is 'a formal principle', not 'that to which being belongs' (p. 38).

Question VI   The Goodness of God

First Article   **Whether to Be Good Belongs to God?**
(pp. 51–2)

Objection 1   To be good does not seem to belong to God, because it relates to 'limit, species and order', but God is none of these things (p. 51).

Obj. 2   The good is 'what all things desire', but they do not all desire God, because they do not know him; and 'nothing is desired unless it is known' (p. 51).

On the contrary, it is written that God is good to those that hope in him.

I answer that, to be good 'belongs pre-eminently to God' (p. 51). God is 'the first producing cause of all things', so the good and desirable 'belong to Him' (p. 51).

Reply Obj. 1   Limitations belong 'to the essence of caused good'. However, good is in God 'as in its cause', so it 'belongs to Him to impose limit, species and order' on them (p. 51).

Reply Obj. 2   All things desire God, by 'desiring their own perfection' (p. 52). Some of the beings desiring God know him as he is in himself; others have 'some **participation** of His goodness'; while others, directed to their ends by a 'higher knower', have a 'natural desire' without knowledge (p. 52).

Second Article   Whether God Is the Highest Good?
(pp. 52–3)

Objection 1   God seems not to be the '*highest* good', because this must add something to good, or it would not be the 'highest good' (p. 52). But something that is an addition is '**composite**' (p. 52). As God is 'supremely simple', he cannot be the highest good (p. 52).

Obj. 2   What everyone desires is 'nothing but God', so 'there is no other good but God'. So, God 'cannot be called the highest good' (p. 52).

Obj. 3   Highest 'implies comparison', but things not in the same genus cannot be compared (p. 52). As God is not in the same genus as 'other good things', he cannot be called 'good in relation to them' (p. 52).

On the contrary, Augustine writes that the Trinity is '*the highest good*' (p. 52).

I answer that, God is 'the highest good absolutely' (p. 52). All 'desired perfections flow from Him as from the first cause'; and not as from a '**univocal agent**', but as from one that 'does not agree with its effects either in species or genus' (p. 52). With a **univocal cause**, the likeness of its effect is 'found uniformly', but, with an '**equivocal**' one, it is 'found more excellently', just as 'heat is in the sun more excellently than it is in fire' (p. 52). As good is in God as the first, not the univocal, 'cause of all things', it must be with him 'more excellently', and he is rightly called 'the highest good' (p. 52).

Reply Obj. 1   What the highest good adds to good is not 'any absolute thing', but a 'relation' (p. 52). This is something 'said of God relatively to **creatures**'; and it is in creatures, but 'in God in our idea only' (p. 52).

Reply Obj. 2   To say that '*good is what all desire*', does not mean that 'every kind of good thing is desired by all', but that what is desired 'has the nature of good' (p. 53). When it is said '*None is good but God*', this refers to the 'essentially good' (p. 53).

Reply Obj. 3   To say that God is 'not of the same genus' with other good things means that he is 'outside genus', as the 'principle of every genus' (p. 53)

Fourth Article   *Whether all Things Are Good by the Divine Goodness? (pp. 54–5)*

Objection 1   All things seem to be 'good by the divine goodness' (p. 54). However, 'everything is good by its own good', so 'everything is good by that very good which is God' (p. 54).

Obj. 2   Everything is 'called good according as they are directed to God', which is 'by reason of the divine goodness' (p. 54). So, 'all things are good by the divine goodness' (p. 54).

On the contrary, all things are good 'inasmuch as they have being' (p. 54).

I answer that, the contrary view is that everything is good by having being, but they are called beings through their own being, not the divine being. Similarly, they are good by their own goodness, not the 'divine goodness' (p. 54).

It was **Plato**'s view that 'the essences of all things' existed separately, and that 'individuals were **denominated** by them as participating in the separate essences' (p. 55). **Socrates**, for example, was called a man 'according to the separate **Form** of man' (p. 55). Plato maintained that there were separate 'Forms of *being* and of *one*', by participating in which, 'everything was called *being* or *one*' (p. 55). Absolute 'being and absolute one' was the 'highest good' and, as good and being are convertible, this was 'the absolute good God', from whom 'all things are called good by way of participation' (p. 55).

It seems 'unreasonable' to maintain the existence of 'separate forms of natural things' (p. 55). But, as Aristotle agrees, there is 'something first', which is 'essentially being and essentially good', and which we call God (p. 55). Therefore, everything can be called good and a being, in so far as it participates, albeit 'distantly and defectively', in the 'first being' (p. 55).

Everything is called good 'from the divine goodness', but it is called good because of the 'likeness of the divine goodness belonging to it' (p. 55). And this is 'formally its own goodness'; so, there is 'one goodness, and yet many goodnesses' (p. 55).

This is a sufficient reply to the objections.

Question VII   The Infinity of God

First Article   Whether God Is Infinite? (pp. 56–7)

Objection 1   It seems that God is 'not infinite', as infinite things are 'imperfect', as they have 'parts and **matter**' (p. 56). God, however, is 'most perfect', and so cannot be infinite (p. 56).

Obj. 2   According to Aristotle, finite and infinite 'belong to quantity', but God is not a body, and there is no quantity in him (p. 56).

Obj. 3   What is one thing in such a way as not to be something else is 'finite according to **substance**' (p. 56). But God is this and not another, so he is 'not infinite in substance' (p. 56).

On the contrary, it has been written that '*God is infinite and eternal and boundless*' (p. 56).

I answer that, The '*ancient philosophers*' attributed '*infinitude to the first principle*', but some of them made the mistake of thinking that matter was the first principle, and concluded that the first principle had '**material infinity**' (p. 56).

Infinity attributed to matter 'has the nature of something imperfect'; it is 'formless matter' (p. 57). Form is not 'made perfect by matter', but is 'contracted' by it (p. 57). The infinite, as 'form not determined by matter', is 'something perfect' (p. 57). Being is the 'most formal of all things' (p. 57). God is not 'a being received in anything', but is 'His own subsistent being', and clearly he is 'infinite and perfect' (p. 57).

This answers the first objection.

Reply Obj. 2   The 'infinite of quantity' is 'in the order of matter', and so cannot be attributed to God (p. 57).

Reply Obj. 3   That God's being is '**self-subsisting**' and called infinite shows that he is 'distinguished from all other beings' (p. 57).

Question IX   The Immutability of God

First Article   Whether God Is Altogether Immutable?
(pp. 70–1)

Objection 1   God seems not to be completely **immutable**, because what 'moves itself' is mutable, and it is said that God moves himself (p. 70).

Obj. 2   God is 'wisdom itself', but this is said to be '*more mobile*' than anything else' (Wisdom 7.24) (p. 70).

Obj. 3   To approach and recede is to move, and, 'in scripture', it says that God does so (p. 70).

On the contrary, it is written that God does not change.

I answer that, God is '**pure act**, without the admixture of any potentiality', which means that he cannot 'change in any way' (p. 70). Further, in everything that moves, there is 'some kind of composition', but God is 'altogether simple', and so cannot be moved (p. 70). Also, whatever moves 'acquires something by its movement', but God is 'infinite', containing 'the perfection of all being', so he cannot do so (pp. 70–1).

Reply Obj. 1   It is possible to call 'every operation', including those of 'understanding and willing', movements; and, in this way, it is said that God 'moves Himself' (p. 71). It does not mean that there is any change in him, as there would be in a thing 'existing in potentiality' (p. 71).

Reply Obj. 2   Wisdom is called 'mobile by way of **similitude**', because nothing can exist, which 'does not proceed from the divine wisdom, by way of some kind of imitation' (p. 71). And, from the 'highest' to the 'lowest' things, there is 'a kind of **procession** and movement of the divine wisdom to things' (p. 71).

Reply Obj. 3   In scripture, things are said of God '**metaphorically**' (p. 71). God is said to approach us in the same way that the sun, as its rays reach it, is said to enter a house (p. 71).

Question X   The Eternity of God

Second Article   Whether God Is Eternal? (pp. 76–7)

Objection 1   God cannot be eternal, because, as **Boethius** has explained, time is made by '*the now that flows away*', and eternity by '*the now that stands still*'; and Augustine has said God is its '*author*' (p. 76).

Obj. 2   God cannot be eternal, because he is said to be before eternity and to reign after it.

Obj. 3   Eternity is a 'kind of measure', but being measured does not belong to God (p. 76).

Obj. 4   There is no past, present or future in eternity but, in scripture, such terms are applied to God.

On the contrary, it has been written that Father, Son and Holy Spirit are eternal.

I answer that, as God is 'immutable', he is 'eternal', and, as he is his own essence, he is 'His own eternity' (p. 76).

Reply Obj. 1   The idea of the now standing still is how we understand eternity, just as we understand time by the idea of 'the flow of the *now*' (p. 76). Augustine is referring to eternity in which we share.

Reply Obj. 2   God is before eternity 'as it is shared by **immaterial substances**' (p. 76). To say that God reigns beyond eternity is a way of saying that he endures 'beyond every kind of given duration' (p. 76).

Reply Obj. 3   Eternity is 'nothing else but God Himself' (p. 77). The idea of measurement does not mean that God is measured, but relates to our understanding of eternity (p. 77).

Reply Obj. 4   Words indicating time are used of God, 'because his eternity includes all times'; he is not affected by 'past, present and future' (p. 77).

Question XII   How God Is Known by Us

First Article   *Whether Any Created Intellect Can See the Essence of God? (pp. 91–3)*

Objection 1   It seems that no '**created intellect**' can see God's essence (p. 91).

Obj. 2   Everything infinite is 'unknown'. God is infinite, and so 'in Himself He is unknown' (p. 91).

Obj. 3   The created intellect 'knows only existing things', but God is 'super-existence', and so is 'above all intellect' (pp. 91–2).

Obj. 4   There must be 'some proportion between the knower and the known', but there is an 'infinite distance' between the created intellect and God (p. 92).

On the contrary, in 1 John 3.2, it states: '*We shall see Him as He is*' (p. 92).

I answer that, as everything is 'knowable according as it is actual', God, as 'pure act', is 'supremely knowable' in himself (p. 92). But what is supremely knowable in itself may not be to a 'particular intellect', because it is so far above it (p. 92).

Some have said that no created intellect can ever see God's essence, but this would mean that no created intellect could 'attain to **beatitude**' (p. 92). A **rational creature**'s '**ultimate perfection**' is to be found in the 'source of its being', and human beings have a 'natural desire' to know the cause of any effect (p. 92). But this natural desire would not be satisfied if they could not 'attain to the first cause of things' (p. 92). So, it must be 'granted absolutely that the blessed see the essence of God' (p. 92).

Reply Obj. 1   Both Dionysius and **Chrysostom** refer to the '**vision of comprehension**' (p. 92).

Reply Obj. 2   The infinity of form, which is not limited by matter, 'is in itself supremely known', and this is the case with God (p. 92).

Reply Obj. 3   It is not that God cannot be known at all, but that he 'transcends all knowledge', which means he is 'not comprehended' (pp. 92–3).

Reply Obj. 4   As far as proportion is concerned, every 'relation of one thing to another is called proportion', so there is proportion of creatures to God: that of effects to their cause (p. 93). And, in this way, 'a created intellect can be proportioned to know God' (p. 93).

Twelfth Article Whether God Can Be Known in this Life by Natural Reason? (pp. 109–10)

Objection 1 Boethius has said that '*reason does not grasp a simple form*', and, as God is a 'supremely simple form', it seems that he cannot be known by natural reason (p. 109).

Obj. 2 The soul 'understands nothing by natural reason without an image', but there cannot be an image of God, 'Who is **incorporeal**' (p. 109).

Obj. 3 Knowledge through natural reason includes 'both good and evil', but knowledge of God 'belongs only to the good' (p. 109).

On the contrary, what can be known of God by natural reason, '*is manifest in them* (Romans 1.19)' (p. 109).

I answer that, natural knowledge 'begins from sense', so it can only extend to '**sensible things**' (p. 109). Sense cannot lead our intellect 'to see the essence of God', because 'sensible creatures are effects of God', and do not equal his power (p. 109).

However, although we cannot know God's 'whole power' from sensible things, because they are God's effects, dependent on him as their cause, we can get as far as knowing that he exists, and that he is 'the first cause of all things', who exceeds all the things he causes (p. 109). Thus, we know his 'relationship with creatures'; that he causes them; that they are different from him, as he is not part of what he causes; and that he '**superexceeds** them all' (p. 109).

Reply Obj. 1 Reason cannot know what a simple form is, but it can know that it is.

Reply Obj. 2 God is known 'by natural knowledge through the images of His effects' (p. 109).

Reply Obj. 3 Knowledge of God's essence comes through 'grace', and is known only to the good, but knowledge of God, through natural reason, is available to the good and the bad (p. 109).

Thirteenth Article   *Whether by Grace a Higher Knowledge of God Can Be Obtained than by Natural Reason? (pp. 110–11)*

Objection 1   It seems that a 'higher knowledge of God' is not attainable by grace than by natural reason (p. 110). **Dionysius** has said that being united to God in this life is as to 'one entirely unknown' (p. 110). But being united to God, but not knowing '*what He is*', is also achievable through natural reason (p. 110).

Obj. 2   We can obtain knowledge of God by natural reason 'only through images', but this is true of knowledge by grace (p. 110).

Obj. 3   Our intellect holds to God 'by the **grace** of faith', but it has been said that things that are not seen are objects of faith, not knowledge; so faith is not knowledge (p. 110).

On the contrary, God has revealed things to us by his Holy Spirit.

I answer that, knowledge from natural reason requires 'images' from sensible things, together with 'a natural intelligible light', so that we can 'abstract' **intelligible concepts** from them (p. 110). With both, the 'revelation of grace' helps human knowledge (p. 110). The '**intellect's natural light**' is assisted by the light of grace, and images 'in the imagination' may be 'divinely formed' (p. 110).

Reply Obj. 1   The 'revelation of grace' may not enable us to know, in this life, what God is, but we get to know him 'more fully', as his effects are 'demonstrated to us'; and there are some things, such as God being '**Three and One**', which are only knowable 'by divine revelation' (p. III).

Reply Obj. 2   The **infusion of divine light** affords us greater understanding of the natural images that we receive from our senses, or which are 'divinely formed in the imagination' (p. III).

Reply Obj. 3   Faith is a 'kind of knowledge', because faith directs the intellect to 'some knowable object' (p. III). But this direction does not come from 'the vision of the believer, but from the vision of Him Who is believed' (p. III).

Question XIII   The Names of God

First Article   Whether a Name Can Be Given to God? (pp. 112–14)

Objection I   It seems that God cannot be given a name. As Dionysius has written: '*Of Him there is neither name, nor can one be found of Him*' (p. 112).

Obj. 2   Concrete names cannot be applied to God, because he is 'simple', and abstract ones cannot be applied because 'they do not signify any perfect subsisting thing' (p. 112).

Obj. 3   Nouns, verbs and pronouns cannot be applied to God, because he has no 'quality, or **accident**, or time', and cannot be 'felt' or 'pointed out' (p. 112).

On the contrary, it says in Exodus 15.3 that God's name is 'Almighty' (p. 113)

I answer that, as Aristotle has shown, words are 'signs of ideas, and ideas the similitudes of things', so clearly words signify things 'through the conception of the intellect' (p. 113). So, we can give a name to anything that we understand. Now, in this life, we cannot see God's essence, but we can know him from creatures as he is their cause. Thus, we can name God from his creatures, but not in the sense that the name used 'expresses the divine essence' in the way that the name, '*man* expresses the essence of man in himself' (p. 113). In the latter case, 'the idea expressed by the name is the definition' (p. 113).

Reply Obj. 1   God is said not to have a name because his essence is 'above all that we understand about God and signify in words' (p. 113).

Reply Obj. 2   As we 'know and name' God from creatures, the names we give to God 'signify what belongs to **material creatures**' (p. 113). And because what is 'perfect and subsistent' in creatures is 'composite', all the names we use of them 'must have a concrete meaning, as befits composite things' (p. 113). In relation to God, we use 'simple and abstract names to signify His **simplicity**', and concrete names 'to signify His subsistence and perfection' (p. 113). However, neither kind of name expresses 'His mode of being', because, in this life, our intellect does not know him as he is (p. 113).

Reply Obj. 3   Verbs and participles signifying time are applied to God, 'because his eternity includes all time' (p. 113). We can only 'apprehend and signify **simple subsistents**' by composite things (p. 113). In the same way, we can only understand and express 'simple eternity' through '**temporal things**' (p. 113). This is because our intellect relates to these things. We can point to God 'only as far as we understand Him' (pp. 113–14).

Second Article   Whether Any Name Can Be Applied to God Substantially? (pp. 114–16)

Objection 1   It seems that no name can be applied to God, because what is said of God cannot '*signify His substance, but rather show forth what He is not*' (p. 114).

Obj. 2   The names applied to God relate to 'processions' from God: they do not signify anything relating to his essence, and so are 'not said of Him substantially' (p. 114).

Obj. 3   We name a thing 'according as we understand it'. However, in this life, we do not understand God 'in His substance', so we cannot apply names 'substantially to God' (p. 114).

On the contrary, Augustine has said that all the names used are applied substantially to God (p. 114).

I answer that, names applied to God 'negatively', or which refer to his relation to creatures, do not signify his substance, but express creatures' distance from him (p. 114). With such names as *'good'* and *'wise'*, there are various views (p. 114). Some say that, although they appear to be applied 'affirmatively' to God, they 'remove something' from him, rather than 'posit' something of him (p. 114). So, to say that God 'lives' is to say that he is not like 'inanimate' things (p. 114). Others argue that the names refer to his relationship with his creatures. To say that God is good is to say that he is 'the cause of goodness in things' (p. 114).

But neither view seems satisfactory. They do not explain why some names, rather than others, should be applied to God. If saying that God is good means only that God causes good things, then it might be said that saying God is the cause of bodies means that he has a body. Further, it would mean that all names were applied to God 'in a secondary sense' (p. 115). Also, this it not what people intend when they speak of God. They mean more, when they say God lives, than that he is the 'the cause of our life', or is not like an inanimate body (p. 115).

So, we must maintain that these names 'signify the **divine substance**', and are 'predicated substantially of God', but fall short of 'representing Him' (p. 115). These names represent God as far as our intellects know him, which, as we know him from creatures, is 'as far as creatures represent Him' (p. 115). And, as God is perfect, creatures represent him in so far as they possess 'some perfection' (p. 115). So, the names signify God's substance imperfectly, just as creatures do (p. 115). When we say, '*God is good*', we do not mean that he causes goodness, or is not evil, but: '*Whatever good we attribute to creatures pre-exists in God*', and in 'a higher way' (p. 115). It is not that God is good as the cause of goodness, but that he 'causes goodness in things because He is good' (p. 115).

Reply Obj. 1   The names used of God do not signify what he is, because they do not express it perfectly; but they do express it 'imperfectly' (p. 115).

Reply Obj. 2   We know and name God on the basis of his processions to creatures, but these names do not signify the processions. Thus, when we say that God lives, we do not mean that life proceeds from God, but signify 'the principle itself of things', insofar as life pre-exists in God: although it does so more fully than we can understand or signify (p. 116).

Reply Obj. 3   We cannot know God's essence in this life, but only as it is 'represented in the perfections of creatures' (p. 116). And this is how the names we use 'signify it' (p. 116).

Third Article   Whether Any Name Can Be Applied to God Properly? (pp. 116–17)

Objection 1   It seems that names are not 'applied properly' to God, because they are taken from creatures, and are therefore used 'metaphorically' (p. 116).

Obj. 2   Such names as '*good*' or '*wise*' are 'more truly denied of God than given to Him'; so these names are not used properly of God (p. 116).

Obj. 3   All 'corporeal names' must be applied to God meta-phorically, because he is 'incorporeal', but they are 'bound up with time and composition' (p. 116).

On the contrary, not all names are applied to God metaphori-cally (p. 116).

I answer that, we know God from 'the perfections which flow from Him' to his creatures (p. 116). We apprehend these per-fections in creatures, and 'signify them by names' (p. 116). When we apply these names to God, we distinguish between the perfections and 'their mode of **signification**' (p. 117). We recognize that what the names signify, such as goodness and life, belong 'primarily' to God, not his creatures; but their mode of signification 'befits creatures', and so does not 'prop-erly and strictly apply to God' (p. 117).

Reply Obj. 1   Some names can only be used of God metaphori-cally, because (as the way creatures receive them has become part of the 'signification of the name itself'), they express the perfections 'flowing from God to creatures' imperfectly (p. 117). However, there are others, such as *'being, good, liv-ing'*, which, because they 'express the perfections themselves absolutely', can be 'applied to God properly' (p. 117).

Reply Obj. 2   The reason such names are denied of God is because they apply to him 'in a more eminent way' than 'the ordinary sense' of their signification (p. 117).

Reply Obj. 3   The names applied to God properly do not 'imply corporeal conditions' in the thing signified, but in the 'mode of signification' (p. 117). Those applied to God metaphorically 'imply and mean a corporeal condition in the thing signified' (p. 117).

Fourth Article   Whether Names Applied to God Are Synonymous? (pp. 117–18)

Objection 1   The names applied to God seem to be 'synonymous', because they 'mean entirely the same thing in God' (p. 117). For example, God's goodness 'is His essence' and so is his wisdom (p. 117).

Obj. 2   It could be argued that the names signify 'the same thing in reality', but different ideas (p. 117). But as there is only one thing, the different ideas seem to be 'empty notions' (p. 117).

Obj. 3   God is 'supremely one', and does not seem to be 'one in reality and many in idea', so the names are synonymous (p. 117).

On the contrary, if all the names used of God are synonymous, 'we cannot properly say *good God*' (p. 118).

I answer that, they are not. Our intellect knows God from creatures and, in order to understand him, forms conceptions, based on the perfections that flow 'from God to creatures' which, although they 'pre-exist in God unitedly and simply', are 'divided and multiplied' as received by creatures (p. 118). Thus, although the names we apply to God 'signify one reality', they are not synonymous, because they do so 'under many and diverse aspects' (p. 118).

This answers the first objection. Synonymous names 'signify one thing under one aspect', but names that signify different aspects of one thing do not 'signify primarily and absolutely one thing' (p. 118).

Reply Obj. 2   The 'many aspects' of these names are not 'useless and empty', because 'one simple reality' corresponds to all of them (p. 118).

Reply Obj. 3   God's 'perfect **unity**' means that what is 'manifold and divided' in other things exists 'simply and unitedly' in him (p. 118). He is one reality, but our intellect 'apprehends Him in a manifold manner' (p. 118).

Fifth Article   Whether what Is Said of God and of Creatures Is Univocally Predicated of Them? (pp. 118–21)

Objection 1   Things 'attributed to God and creatures' seem to be '**univocal**', as every '**equivocal** term' is reduced to a univocal one (p. 118). For example, the name 'dog' can be used equivocally of both the barking dog and the dogfish, but it must be used of one (the barking dog) univocally, or 'we proceed to infinitude' (pp. 118–19).

Obj. 2   No likeness is 'understood through equivocal names' (p. 119). As creatures bear a 'certain likeness to God', it seems that something can be said of 'God and creatures univocally' (p. 119).

Obj. 3   As God is the 'first measure of all beings', he must be '**homogeneous**' with his creatures, and so a name may be applied univocally to both (p. 119).

On the contrary, what is predicated of different things 'under the same name but not in the same sense' is predicated equivocally (p. 119). Any names belong to God and creatures in different senses. Wisdom, for example, is 'a quality' in creatures, but not in God (p. 119). Also, the distance between God and creatures is greater than that between any creatures, but the distance between some creatures rules out univocal predication. So this is even less possible of God and creatures.

I answer that, the reason that univocal predication between God and creatures is impossible is that every effect, which is not 'a proportioned result' of its cause, 'falls short' of it (p. 119). The perfections existing in creatures are 'divided and multiplied', whereas, in God, they pre-exist 'unitedly' (p. 119). So, for example, when we say that a man is wise, it 'comprehends' the thing signified (pp. 119–20). However, when the name is applied to God, it does not, because God exceeds 'the signification of the name' (p. 120). Therefore, no name is 'predicated univocally of God and of creatures' (p. 120).

But the names are not applied to them equivocally either, because otherwise nothing could be 'known or demonstrated' about God from creatures (p. 120). The names are used of God and creatures in 'an **analogous** sense', which is 'according to proportion' (p. 120).

This means that whatever is said of God and creatures is 'according as there is some relation of the creature to God as to its principle and cause', in whom 'all the perfections of things pre-exist excellently' (p. 120). With analogies, the idea is not, as it is when something is said univocally, 'one and the same', nor is it 'totally diverse', as when it is said equivocally (p. 120).

Reply Obj. 1   The universal cause of the whole species is not a 'univocal agent', and the universal cause comes before the particular (p. 120). But the 'universal agent', although not univocal, is 'not altogether equivocal', for otherwise it could not 'produce its own likeness' (p. 120). It can still be called an 'analogical agent', just as, in predications, 'all univocal names are reduced to the first non-univocal analogical name, which is *being*' (pp. 120–21).

Reply Obj. 2   Creatures' 'likeness' to God is 'imperfect', because they do not represent 'the same thing even generically' (p. 121).

Reply Obj. 3   God is not 'a measure proportioned to the things measured', so God and creatures do not need to be 'in the same genus' (p. 121).

Sixth Article   Whether Names Predicated of God Are Predicated Primarily of Creatures? (pp. 121–2)

Objection 1   As we 'know creatures before we know God', it seems that the names we use 'are predicated primarily of creatures rather than of God' (p. 121).

Obj. 2   Names 'transferred from creatures to God', such as '*lion*' and '*stone*', refer primarily to creatures, not God (p. 121).

Obj. 3   Names applied to both God and creatures apply to God as '*the cause of all creatures*' (p. 121). But what is applied to the cause of something is 'applied to it secondarily' (p. 121).

On the contrary, the names are applied primarily to God.

I answer that, when names are used analogically, they 'are predicated through a relation to some one thing', which must be put in the definition of all of them (p. 121).

And, as the '*essence expressed by the name is the definition*', the name must apply 'primarily to that which is put in the definition of the other things', and secondarily to the others as they approximate to the first (p. 121).

All names 'applied metaphorically' to God apply primarily to creatures, because 'they mean only similitudes to such creatures' (p. 122). For example, when the word '*lion*' is applied to God, it means that God shows 'strength in His works', as a lion does (p. 122). With other names applied to God, the same would be the case only if they referred to God 'as the cause' (p. 122). So, '*God is good*' or '*wise*' would mean that 'God causes his creatures' goodness' (p. 122). However, such names are applied to God, not just as the cause, but 'essentially', signifying that these perfections exist in God 'in a more excellent way' (p. 122). The names apply primarily to God, because 'these perfections flow from God to creatures' (p. 122). However, with the 'imposition of the names', we apply them primarily to creatures, 'which we know first' (p. 122).

Reply Obj. 1   This objection is true to the extent that it applies to the 'imposition of the name' (p. 122).

Reply Obj. 2   The same rule does not apply to 'metaphorical and other names' (p. 122).

Reply Obj. 3   This would be valid only if the names applied to God 'as cause, and not also essentially' (p. 122).

Twelfth Article   Whether Affirmative Propositions Can Be Formed About God? (pp. 132–4)

Objection 1   This seems not to be possible. As Dionysius has pointed out, '*negations about God are true; but affirmations are vague*' (p. 132).

Obj. 2   Everything in relation to which 'an **affirmative proposition** is made' is a subject (p. 132). However, a simple form 'cannot be a subject', but God is 'most absolutely a simple form' (p. 132).

Obj. 3   God has no 'composition', but to make an affirmation about something is to understand it as 'composite' (p. 132).

On the contrary, what comes from faith cannot be false, and such propositions as 'God is Three and One' are **affirmative propositions of faith** (p. 132).

I answer that, there are 'affirmative propositions of faith', such as that God is '**Three and One**' and 'omnipotent' (p. 132). And, indeed, affirmative propositions can be made about God. With 'every true affirmative proposition', subject and predicate must, in some way, signify 'the same thing in reality', but 'diverse things in idea' (p. 133). Thus, when it is said that, '*man is an animal*', 'predicate and subject are the same as to **suppositum**, but diverse as to idea': there is both a sensible nature (so he is an animal) and a rational one (so he is a man) (p. 133). God is 'one and simple', but, because we cannot see him as he is in himself, we know him 'according to diverse conceptions': although we also know that only one reality 'corresponds to' these conceptions (p. 133).

Reply Obj. 1   Dionysius' point is that what is affirmed of God is 'vague', because 'no name can be applied to God according to its mode of signification' (p. 133).

Reply Obj. 2   We cannot 'apprehend simple subsisting forms' as they are in themselves, but only in 'the manner of composite things' (p. 133).

Reply Obj. 3   When an intellect understands something to be other than it is, it is false. But this is not the case here, because our intellect, when it forms a proposition about God, does affirm that he is 'simple' (p. 133). However our intellect understands in one way, but 'things are in another' (p. 134). We understand **material things** in an 'immaterial way' and 'simple things' in a 'composite' way. However, we do not think that they are 'composite things', so our intellect 'is not false in composing a judgment' about God (p. 134).

Question XXV   The Power of God

Second Article   Whether the Power of God Is Infinite? (pp. 260–2)

Objection 1   God's power seems not to be infinite, for, according to Aristotle, everything infinite is 'imperfect'; but God's power is not (p. 260).

Obj. 2   Every power is 'made known by its effect'. If God's power is infinite, it would 'produce an infinite effect', which is impossible (p. 260).

Obj. 3   Aristotle proves that a 'corporeal thing' with infinite power would 'cause movement instantaneously' (p. 261). But God does not, so he does not have infinite power (p. 261).

On the contrary, God is said to be 'infinite' (p. 261).

I answer that, God's being is infinite, so his **active power** 'should be infinite' (p. 261). The 'more perfectly an **agent** has the form by which it acts, the greater its power to act' (p. 261). As the 'divine essence, through which God acts, is infinite', so is his power (p. 261).

Reply Obj. 1   Aristotle is referring to 'an infinity belonging to matter not limited by any form', which belongs to quantity (p. 261). This is not how 'the divine essence' is, and so God's power is infinite (p. 261). So, God's power is not 'imperfect' (p. 261).

Reply Obj. 2   A univocal agent's power is 'wholly manifested in its effect', but God is not a univocal agent, so his effect is 'always less than His power' (p. 261). Therefore, God's infinite power does not have to be 'manifested in the production of an infinite effect' (p. 261). God's power is not 'ordered towards its effect as towards an end', but is 'the end of the effect produced by it' (p. 261).

Reply Obj. 3   Aristotle was referring to a 'univocal agent', whose whole power would be 'made manifest in its motion' (p. 262). But the whole of an 'incorporeal' agent's power would not be 'manifested in motion', although it would be motion in 'null time' (p. 262).

Third Article   Whether God Is Omnipotent? (pp. 262–3)

Objection 1   Everything has 'movement and passiveness', but not God, because he is 'immovable' (p. 262). So, God is not 'omnipotent'.

Obj. 2   Sin is a kind of act, but is not possible for God, so he is not omnipotent.

Obj. 3   God is said to show his omnipotence particularly in '*sparing and having* **mercy**' (p. 262). But there are 'greater' acts than these, such as creating 'another world' (p. 262). So, God is not omnipotent.

Obj. 4 If God were omnipotent, everything would be possible, and nothing impossible. But if the impossible is removed, so, too, is 'the necessary': for 'what necessarily exists cannot possibly not exist' (p. 262). So, 'if God were omnipotent', there would be nothing necessary (p. 262). However, as this is impossible, God is 'not omnipotent' (p. 262).

On the contrary, no word is impossible with God.

I answer that, everybody acknowledges God's omnipotence, but it is hard to explain what it is. If we think about it, to say, '*God can do all things*' means all possible things (p. 263). Aristotle has explained that there are two ways in which something is possible. First, things are possible 'in relation to some power' as, for example, that of human beings (p. 263). But God's omnipotence cannot relate to what is 'possible to created nature' (p. 263). And if we say that it relates to being able to do the things possible to divine power, we get a 'vicious circle' (p. 263).

So, is God omnipotent because he is able to do 'all things that are possible absolutely' (p. 263)? Things are possible absolutely if 'the predicate is not incompatible with the subject', as in 'Socrates sits', and impossible absolutely if it is, as in 'that man is an ass' (p. 263).

Every agent 'produces an effect like itself', and so 'to each active power there corresponds a thing possible as its proper object according to the nature of that act on which its active power is founded' (p. 263). But the 'divine being' is infinite, possessing 'the perfection of all being' (p. 263). Thus, anything with 'the nature of being' is among the 'absolute possibles', in relation to which God is omnipotent (p. 263).

Non-being is the only thing 'opposed to the notion of being' (p. 263). Something involving 'being and non-being' is not absolutely possible, and 'cannot come under the divine omnipotence' (p. 263). This is not because God's power is defective, but because it is not possible. Thus, God's omnipotence extends to everything which does not involve a '**contradiction in terms**' (p. 263).

Reply Obj. 1   God is omnipotent 'in respect to active power', so his omnipotence is not incompatible with his immovability (p. 264).

Reply Obj. 2   God cannot sin, as this would be 'to fall short of a perfect action' (p. 264). But Aristotle has said that God can *deliberately do what is evil*' (p. 264). But either this must be understood as part of a **conditional proposition**, which can be true, even though 'the **antecedent** and **consequent** are impossible', as in 'If a man is an ass, he has four feet'; or he meant that God can do things that seem evil now; or he is speaking as a **pagan**, believing that 'men became gods' (p. 264).

Reply Obj. 3   God's omnipotence is shown especially in having mercy, because he thus 'freely forgives sins'; and it is not the prerogative of an **inferior power** to do so (p. 264). By showing them mercy, he leads them to sharing in 'an infinite good', which is 'the ultimate effect of the divine power' (p. 264).

Reply Obj. 4   What is said to be possible for some power is said to be so 'in reference to its **proximate cause**' (p. 264). The things which God does are said 'to be possible in reference to a higher cause' (p. 264). It is the 'condition of the proximate cause' that determines whether the 'effect has **contingency** or necessity' (p. 264). And so the world, in its foolishness, concludes that what is impossible for nature is so for God. However, God's omnipotence does not remove from things 'their impossibility and necessity' (p. 264).

Fifth Article   Whether God Can Do what He Does not?
(pp. 266–8)

Objection 1   As God 'cannot do what He has not **foreknown**
and **pre-ordained** that He would do', he can only do what he
does (p. 266).

Obj. 2   God can 'only do what ought to be done and what is
just', and is not 'bound' to do anything else (p. 266).

Obj. 3   God cannot do anything that would harm creation,
and it would not be good for creatures to be 'otherwise than
as they are' (p. 266).

On the contrary, God can do what he does not.

I answer that, in considering this question, some people make
the mistake of thinking that God 'acts from natural necessity', so that nothing can happen except what actually does
(p. 266). However, this is not the case: God's will is 'the cause
of all things' (p. 266). So, there is no 'necessity' in the **present
scheme of things**', such that other things 'could not come to
be' (p. 267).

Others have argued that things must be as they are, due to
'divine wisdom and justice, without which God does nothing'
(p. 267). But the divine wisdom, which has established the
order of creation, is not 'restricted to it' (p. 267). The created
order is not equal to God's wisdom, from which a different
'scheme of things' could have proceeded (p. 267). So, God
'can do other things than those He has done' (p. 267).

Reply Obj. 1   God's 'power, essence, will, intellect, wisdom
and justice are one and the same' (p. 267). Thus, there is
nothing in his power that is not also 'found in His just will or
in His wise intellect'; so there is nothing to stop there being
'something in the divine power which He does not will, and
which is not included in the order that He has established in
things' (p. 267). By his '**absolute power**', God could do differ-

ent things from those he 'has foreknown and pre-ordained to do'; but he could not do anything that he has not foreknown and pre-ordained to do (pp. 267–8). His doing is 'subject to His foreknowledge and pre-ordination', but his power, which is his nature, is not (p. 268). God does things because he so wills, but is able to do so, not 'because He so wills, but because He is such in His nature' (p. 268).

Reply Obj. 2   When it is said that God 'can do only what He ought', all this means is that he can only do 'what is for Him fitting and just' (p. 268). But this does not mean that God can only do 'what is now fitting and just', as reflected in the 'present order of things' (p. 268). It means that: '*God cannot do anything except that which, if He did it, would be suitable and just*' (p. 268).

Reply Obj. 3   The present order is restricted to what now exists, but God's 'power and wisdom' are not (p. 268). Another order would not be 'suitable and good' for things existing now, but God could 'make other things and impose upon them another order' (p. 268).

Overview

The following section is a chapter-by-chapter overview of Aquinas' *Summa Theologica* (God, Part I), designed for quick reference to the detailed summary above. Readers may also find this overview section helpful for revision.

God (Part I)

Question 1   The Nature and Domain of Sacred Doctrine

First Article   Whether, Besides the Philosophical Disciplines, Any Further Doctrine Is Required? (pp. 5–6)

The objections are:

- only philosophy is required, as human beings should not seek knowledge that is above reason;
- issues concerning God are covered by philosophy.

Aquinas' answer is: sacred doctrine, which is revealed by God, is needed, because it is the only way that truths that are beyond human reason can be known. Further, only a few understand the truths about God that can be known through reason.

His replies to the objections are:

- revelation must be accepted through faith, and these are the things with which sacred doctrine deals;
- different disciplines can establish the same truths in different ways, so philosophy and theology can cover the same issues.

Question II   The Existence of God

First Article   Whether the Existence of God Is Self-Evident?
(pp. 18–20)

The objections are:

- God's existence seems self-evident, because it exists in us naturally;
- once the term 'God' is understood, it is seen that the proposition, 'God exists' is self-evident, because, as that than which nothing greater can be conceived, God must exist, as actual existence is greater than merely mental existence;
- truth's existence is self-evident and, as truth itself, God's existence is self-evident.

Aquinas' answer is: something can be self-evident in two ways: in itself and not to us, and in itself and to us. In a self-evident proposition, the predicate is included in the essence of the subject, as in 'Man is an animal'. So, if the essence of both predicate and subject are known, the proposition will be self-evident. If not, the proposition will be self-evident in itself, but not to those who do not know the meaning of predicate and subject. 'God exists' is not self-evident because, as God is his own existence, subject and predicate are the same. Not knowing God's essence, the proposition is not self-evident to us, but needs to be proved from things better known to us: his effects (the world God has made and the things it contains).

His replies to the objections are:

- nature gives us general knowledge of God's existence, but not absolute knowledge;
- not all understand the term 'God' to signify something than which nothing greater can be thought and, if they do,

might not understand it to signify something with actual, rather than merely mental, existence, so it cannot be argued that God actually exists (unless it is admitted that there actually exists something than which nothing greater can be thought, which those denying God's existence do not admit);

- the existence of truth in general is self-evident to us, but not that of a Primal Truth.

Second Article   Whether It Can Be Demonstrated that God Exists? (pp. 20–1)

The objections are:

- it seems that God's existence cannot be demonstrated, as it is an article of faith that God exists, and matters of faith cannot be demonstrated, as to do so would produce scientific knowledge;
- we cannot know what God's essence is, only what it is not;
- any demonstration of God's existence would be from his effects, but these are finite, whereas he is infinite, and a cause cannot be demonstrated by an effect that is not in proportion to it.

Aquinas' answer is: there are two kinds of demonstration: through the cause and through the effect. When an effect is better known than its cause, we move from the effect to the cause. As every effect depends upon its cause, if the effect exists, the cause must pre-exist it. God's existence is not self-evident to us, but can be demonstrated from his effects.

His replies to the objections are:

- God's existence can be proved by natural reason, and is not an article of faith, but those unable to understand the proof can accept it on faith;

- when a cause is demonstrated from an effect, the effect takes the place of the cause in proving the cause's existence, and this is particularly so with God;
- perfect knowledge cannot be obtained from effects that are not in proportion to the cause, but the actual existence of the cause can be demonstrated from its effects, and this is so with God.

Third Article   Whether God Exists? (pp. 21–4)

The objections are:

- God seems not to exist, because if one of two contraries is infinite, the other would be destroyed, and God is supposed to be infinitely good, but there is evil in the world;
- it appears that what is in the world can be accounted for without God, as natural things can be explained by nature, while human decisions are the result of human reason.

Aquinas' answer is: God's existence can be proved in five ways.

First way: some things are in motion, and what moves is moved by something else. But this can only be done by something in a state of actuality, as when fire, which is actually hot, makes wood, which is potentially so, actually hot. Now, what is actually hot cannot be potentially so at the same time. Nothing can be mover and moved at the same time, as nothing can move itself. Whatever is moved must be moved by something else. But if this continued to infinity, there would be no first, or any other, mover, so there must be a first mover, moved by no other, which is God.

Second way: there is an order of efficient causes, and nothing is its own efficient cause, because, to be so, it would have to be prior to itself. It is impossible for efficient causes to go on to infinity, because the first cause causes the intermediate one, and that the ultimate cause. To remove the cause is to remove the effect, so, without a first cause, there would be no other causes. But proceeding to infinity would give no first efficient cause, and no intermediate or ultimate effects, so there must be a first efficient cause: God.

Third way: from possibility and necessity. Things in nature could be or not be, so they cannot always have existed, because that which can not-be at some time is not. If everything were of this kind, there would be a time when nothing existed. But then, even now nothing would exist, because nothing would have begun to exist. So, not all things are merely possible; there must exist something that has necessary existence. The necessity of every necessary thing is either caused by something else or it is not. However, as with efficient causes, it is impossible to go to infinity with necessary things, whose necessity is caused by something else. So, there must be something that has of itself its own necessity: God.

Fourth way: things are more or less good. But 'more' and 'less' are 'predicated of different things', to the extent that they resemble a maximum, such as hottest. The maximum in any genus is the cause of all that belongs to it, as fire causes all hot things. Thus, there must be something, which, for all beings, causes their being, goodness, and every other perfection: God.

Fifth way: from the way the world is governed. Things that lack knowledge still act, clearly in a designed way, for an end, so as to obtain the best result. But, as they lack knowledge, an intelligent being must direct them towards their end, just as the archer does an arrow. There must be an intelligent being directing natural things to their end: God.

His replies to the objections are:

- God is the highest good, so would not allow evil in the world, unless through his omnipotence and infinite goodness, he could bring good out of it;
- whatever happens in nature must be traced back to God as first cause, and what is done by human decision must be traced back to a higher cause than human will: an immovable and self-necessary first principle.

Question III   On the Simplicity of God

First Article   Whether God Has a Body? (pp. 25–7)

The objections are:

- God seems to have a body, as the Bible refers to his having three dimensions;
- he seems to have a figure, as the Bible refers to human beings being made in his image;
- in the Bible, God is said to have bodily parts;
- the Bible suggests God has posture;
- the Bible states that people should come to God, as if he were a physical destination.

Aquinas' answer is: there are three ways of showing that God is not a body. A body only moves if moved, but God, as first mover, is himself unmoved. God, as the first being, must necessarily be in act, not potentiality, and so cannot have any potentiality, or be a body. He is the most noble of beings, but a body cannot be.

His replies to the objections are:

- the Bible likens spiritual beings to physical things, because height, for example, can indicate God's transcendence;
- it is human beings' reason and intellect, not their bodies, which are made in God's image;
- in the Bible, saying God has bodily parts is a convenient way of highlighting his actions;
- when God is said to have posture, as in sitting, this indicates his unchangeableness;
- saying that people come to God indicates coming to him spiritually, not physically.

Question IV   The Perfection of God

First Article   Whether God Is Perfect? (pp. 37–8)

The objections are:

- God seems not to be perfect, because a thing is said to be perfect, if completely made, but God is not made;
- God is the first beginning of things, but the beginning of things (such as a seed) seems imperfect;
- God's essence is being itself, but being seems imperfect.

Aquinas' answer is: some ancient philosophers did not predicate 'best' and 'most perfect' of the first principle, because they thought only in terms of a material principle. This would be very imperfect, as it would be absolutely potential. God is not material, but the most actual and perfect first principle.

His replies to the objections are:

- things that come to be are called perfect, when brought from potentiality into actuality, and the term signifies, by extension, whatever is not lacking in actual being;

- the imperfect material principle cannot be absolutely first, but is preceded by something perfect;
- being is the most perfect of all things, because nothing has actuality except in so far as it is, so being is the actuality of all things.

Question VI   The Goodness of God

First Article   **Whether to Be Good Belongs to God?**
(pp. 51–5)

The objections are:

- being good does not seem to belong to God, because it relates to limit, species and order, but God is not these things;
- the good is what all things desire, but they do not all desire God, because they do not know him.

Aquinas' answer is: to be good belongs pre-eminently to God, because he is the first cause of all things, so the good and desirable belong to him.

His replies to the objections are:

- limitations belong to the essence of caused good, but good is in God as in its cause, so it is for him to impose limit, species and order on things;
- all things desire God, by desiring their own perfection. Some of these know God as he is in himself, some participate in his goodness, while others are directed to their ends by God, and have a natural desire but without knowledge.

Second Article   *Whether God Is the Highest Good?*
(pp. 52–3)

The objections are:

- God seems not to be the highest good, as being highest adds something to good, but an addition is composite and, as God is supremely simple, he cannot be the highest good;
- what everyone desires is nothing but God, so there is no other good but God, so God cannot be called the highest good;
- highest implies comparison, but things in the same genus cannot be compared and, as God is not in the same genus as other good things, he cannot be called good in relation to them.

Aquinas' answer is: with a univocal cause, its effects are uniformly like it, but God, who is the highest good absolutely, is an equivocal, not a univocal, cause. God is the highest good absolutely. All desired perfections come from him as the first cause, and he is unlike his effects. Good is in God to the highest degree, so he is rightly called the highest good.

His replies to the objections are:

- when it is said that God is the highest good, this does not add to his goodness: it is a way of referring to God relative to his creatures;
- when it is said that there is no other good but God, this refers to the essentially good;
- to say that God is not in the same genus as other good things means that, as the principle of every genus, he is outside genus.

Fourth Article   Whether all Things Are Good by the Divine Goodness? (pp. 54–5)

The objections are:

- all things seem to be good by the divine goodness;
- everything is called good as it is directed to God, which is by the divine goodness.

Aquinas' answer is: that the contrary view is that everything is good by having being, but is called being through its own, not the divine, being, and so is good by its own, not the divine, goodness. Plato's view was that the essences of all things existed separately, so Socrates was called a man by participation in the separate form of man. There were separate forms of being and one, by participation in which, everything was called being or one. Absolute being and absolute one was the highest good and, as good and being are convertible, this was God, from whom all things are called good by participation. It seems unreasonable to maintain the existence of separate forms of natural things, but Aristotle accepts that there is something first, God, which is essentially being and good. So, everything can be called good and a being, to the extent that it participates in the first being. Thus, everything is called good from the divine goodness, but because of its likeness to the divine goodness, this is formally its own goodness. So, there is one goodness, and yet many goodnesses.

His reply to the objections is: that the above is sufficient.

Question VII   The Infinity of God

First Article   Whether God Is Infinite? (pp. 56–7)

The objections are:

- God seems not to be infinite, as infinite things are imperfect, by having parts and matter so, as God is most perfect, he cannot be infinite;
- finite and infinite belong to quantity but, as God is not a body, he has no quantity;
- what is one thing in such a way as not to be something else is finite according to substance, but God is this and not another, so he is not infinite in substance.

Aquinas' answer is: ancient philosophers attributed infinitude to the first principle, but mistakenly thought that matter was the first principle, and that it had material infinity. Infinite matter is imperfect, as it is formless matter. Form is not made perfect by matter, but is contracted by it, whereas the infinite, as form not determined by matter, is perfect. Being is the most formal of all things. God is not a being received in anything, but is his own subsistent being, and is infinite and perfect.

His replies to the objections are:

- the above answers the first objection;
- infinite of quantity is in the order of matter, and cannot be attributed to God;
- God's being is self-subsisting and being called infinite shows that he is distinguished from all other beings.

Overview

Question IX   The Immutability of God

First Article   Whether God Is Altogether Immutable?
(pp. 70–1)

The objections are:

- God seems not to be completely immutable, because what moves itself is mutable, and God is said to move himself;
- God is wisdom itself, but this is said to be more mobile than anything else;
- in the Bible, it says that God moves.

Aquinas' answer is: God is pure act, without potentiality, meaning he cannot change in any way. In everything that moves, there is some kind of composition, but God is altogether simple, and so cannot be moved. Whatever moves acquires something by its movement, but God is infinite, containing the perfection of all being, so cannot do so. As the first principle, he is immovable.

His replies to the objections are:

- every operation, including those of understanding and willing, can be called movements, and this is how God is said to move himself;
- wisdom is called 'mobile' metaphorically, because nothing can exist that does not proceed from the divine wisdom;
- in the Bible, things are said of God metaphorically.

Question X   The Eternity Of God

Second Article   Whether God Is Eternal? (pp. 76–7)

The objections are:

- God cannot be eternal, because eternity is made by the now that stands still, and God is its author;
- God cannot be eternal, because he is said to be before and after eternity;
- eternity is a kind of measure, but God is not measured;
- eternity has no past, present or future, but, in the Bible, such terms are applied to God.

Aquinas' answer is: God is immutable and eternal and, as he is his own essence, he is his own eternity.

His replies to the objections are:

- the idea of the now standing still is how we understand eternity;
- God being before and after eternity is a way of saying that he endures beyond every kind of given duration;
- eternity is God himself, and the idea of measurement does not mean that God is measured, but is how we understand eternity;
- words indicating time are used of God, because his eternity includes all times, and he is not affected by past, present and future.

Question XII   How God Is Known by Us

First Article   Whether Any Created Intellect Can See the Essence of God? (pp. 91–3)

The objections are:

- no created intellect seems able to see God's essence;
- everything infinite is unknown so, as God is infinite, he is unknown;
- the created intellect knows only existing things but, as God is super-existence, he is above all intellects;
- there must be proportion between knower and known, but there is an infinite distance between the created intellect and God.

Aquinas' answer is: as everything is knowable according as it is actual, God, as pure act, is supremely knowable in himself, but not to a particular intellect, because he is so far above it. Some have said no created intellect can ever see God's essence, but this would mean that created intellects could not attain beatitude. Rational creatures' ultimate perfection is to be found in the source of their being, and they naturally desire to know the cause of any effect. But this desire would not be satisfied if they could not reach the first cause of things, so the blessed must be able to see God's essence.

His replies to the objections are:

- Christian teachers refer to the vision of understanding;
- the infinity of form, which is not limited by matter, is in itself supremely known, and this is the case with God;
- it is not that God cannot be known, but that he transcends all knowledge, which means he is not comprehended;
- there is proportion of creatures to God, that of effects to their cause, and this is how a created intellect can be proportioned to know God.

Twelfth Article   Whether God Can Be Known in this Life by Natural Reason? (pp. 109–10)

The objections are:

- reason does not grasp a simple form and, as God is a supremely simple form, it seems he cannot be known by natural reason;
- the soul understands nothing by natural reason without an image, but there can be no image of God, who has no body;
- knowledge through natural reason includes both good and evil, but knowledge of God is only good.

Aquinas' answer is: natural knowledge starts with the senses, so can only extend to sensible things. The senses cannot lead our intellect to see God's essence, because sensible creatures are God's effects, and do not equal his power. However, although we cannot know God's whole power from sensible things, which depend on him as their cause, we can at least know from them that he exists, and is the first cause of all things, who exceeds all the things he causes, and that his creatures are different from him.

His replies to the objections are:

- reason cannot know what a simple form is, but it can know that it is;
- God is known by natural knowledge through his effects;
- knowledge of God's essence comes through grace, and is known only to the good, but knowledge of God, through natural reason, is available to the good and the bad.

Thirteenth Article   *Whether by Grace a Higher Knowledge of God Can Be Obtained than by Natural Reason?* *(pp. 110–11)*

The objections are:

- it does not seem to be so, because it has been said that being united to God in this life is as to one entirely unknown, and this is achievable through natural reason;
- knowledge of God through natural reason is only through images, but this is true of knowledge by grace;
- it has been said that the things not seen are objects of faith, not knowledge, so faith is not knowledge.

Aquinas' answer is: when acquiring knowledge through natural reason, the natural light of the intellect is assisted by the light of grace, and images in the imagination may be divinely formed.

His replies to the objections are:

- the revelation of grace may not enable us to know what God is, in this life, but we do learn something about him through his effects, while there are some things, such as his being Three and One, which can only be known through revelation;
- divine light gives us greater understanding of the natural images we receive from our senses, or which are divinely formed in the imagination;
- faith is a kind of knowledge, because it directs the intellect to some knowable object, but this direction does not come from the believer, but from God.

Question XIII   The Names of God

First Article   *Whether a Name Can Be Given to God?* *(pp. 112–14)*

The objections are:

- it seems that God does not have a name;
- concrete names cannot be used, because God is simple, while abstract ones do not signify a perfect subsisting thing;
- nouns, verbs and pronouns cannot be used, because God has no quality, accident or time, and cannot be felt or pointed out.

Aquinas' answer is: human beings give names to things they understand. In this life, they cannot see God's essence, but can know him from creatures, as he causes them. God can be named from creatures, but not in the sense that the name expresses the divine essence in the way that 'man' expresses the essence of man in himself.

His replies to the objections are:

- God is said not to have a name, because his essence is above all that human beings can understand and can signify in words;
- God is known from creatures, so the names given to God relate to physical creatures but, because what is perfect and subsistent in creatures is composite, all the names have a concrete meaning: abstract names signify his simplicity, and concrete ones his subsistence and perfection, but neither expresses his mode of being because, in this life, the human intellect does not know him as he is;
- words signifying time are applied to God, because his eternity includes all time, and human beings can only understand and express eternity through temporal things.

Second Article   Whether Any Name Can Be Applied to God Substantially? (pp. 114–16)

The objections are:

- what is said of God only shows what he is not;
- names applied to God relate to processions from God, and, as they do not signify anything relating to his essence, are not said of him substantially;
- things are named as they are understood, but, in this life, God is not understood in his substance, so names cannot be applied substantially to him.

Aquinas' answer is: names applied to God negatively, or which refer to his relation to creatures, do not signify his substance, but express creatures' distance from him. Some say that such names as 'good' or 'wise', although they appear to be applied affirmatively to God, say what he is not, rather that what he is: so to say he 'lives' indicates his not being like inanimate things. Others say that the names refer to his relationship with creatures, so to say God is 'good' means that he causes goodness in things. Neither view explains why some names, but not others, should be applied to God. If God's being good means that he causes good things, then saying God is the cause of bodies means that he has a body. It would mean that all names were applied to God in a secondary sense, and this is not what people think they are doing when they speak of God. So, these names do signify the divine substance, and are predicated of God substantially, but only represent God as far as our intellects know him, which is from creatures. As God is perfect, creatures represent him in so far as they possess some perfection, and so the names signify God's substance imperfectly. Thus, to say God is 'good' is to say that whatever good is attributed to creatures exists in God to a higher degree.

His replies to the objections are:

- names used of God do not signify what he is, as they do not express it perfectly, but they do express it imperfectly;
- God is named and known on the basis of his creatures, but the names do not signify the creatures. To say that God lives does not mean that life proceeds from God, but signifies the principle itself of things, in so far as life pre-exists in God;
- God's essence cannot be known in this life, but only as it is represented in the perfections of creatures, and this is how the names we use signify it.

Third Article   Whether Any Name Can Be Applied to God Properly? (pp. 116–17)

The objections are:

- names seem not to be applied properly to God, because they are taken from creatures, and used metaphorically;
- names like 'good' or 'wise' are more accurately denied of God than given to him;
- all corporeal names must be applied to God metaphorically, because he is incorporeal.

Aquinas' answer is: God is known from the perfections flowing from him to creatures, which are known in creatures, and signified by names. When the names are applied to God, the perfections and the way they are signified are distinguished. What the names signify, such as goodness and life, belong primarily to God, not creatures, but the way they are signified befits creatures, and does not properly apply to God.

His replies to the objections are:

- some names can only be used of God metaphorically

because, as the way creatures receive them has become part of the meaning of the names, they express the perfections flowing from God to creatures imperfectly. Others, such as 'being', 'good' and 'living', express the perfections themselves absolutely, and can be applied to God properly;

- such names are denied of God, because they apply to him in a more eminent way than to creatures;
- names applied to God properly do not imply physical conditions in the thing signified, but in the usual meaning of the name. Those applied to God metaphorically imply and mean a corporeal condition in the thing signified.

Fourth Article   Whether Names Applied to God Are Synonymous? (pp. 117–18)

The objections are:

- names applied to God seem to be synonymous, because they mean the same thing in God, as in God's goodness, which is his essence;
- the names could signify the same thing in reality, but different ideas although, as there is only one thing, having different ideas seems pointless;
- God is supremely one, and does not seem to be one in reality and many in idea, so the names are synonymous.

Aquinas' answer is: the human intellect knows God from creatures and, to understand him, forms ideas, based on the perfections flowing from God to creatures which, although they pre-exist in God unitedly and simply, are divided and multiplied in creatures. So, although the names, when applied to God, signify one reality, they are not synonymous, because they refer to that reality under different aspects.

His replies to the objections are:

- the above answers the first;
- although one simple reality corresponds to all the ideas, they are not pointless;
- God's perfect unity means that what is many and divided in creatures exists simply and unitedly in him, but our intellect understands him through different ideas.

Fifth Article   Whether what Is Said of God and of Creatures Is Univocally Predicated of Them? (pp. 118–21)

The objections are:

- things attributed to God and creatures seem to be univocal, as every equivocal term is reduced to a univocal one;
- no likeness is understood through equivocal names, and because creatures bear some likeness to God, it seems that something can be said of both univocally;
- God is the first measure of all beings, so he must be homogeneous with his creatures, and so a name may be applied univocally to both.

Aquinas' answer is: univocal predication between God and creatures is impossible, because every effect, which is not a proportioned result of its cause, falls short of it. Perfections in creatures are divided and multiplied but, in God, they pre-exist unitedly. So, when a man is said to be wise, the word comprehends the thing it indicates, but it does not in relation to God, because God exceeds what the term signifies. However, the names are not applied to them equivocally either. If they were, nothing could be known or proved about God from creatures. The names are used of God and creatures analogously, which means that what is said of God and creatures is on the basis that creatures are related to God, who is their cause. With analogies, the idea is not one and the same, nor is it totally different.

His replies to the objections are:

- God, the universal agent, although not univocal, is not altogether equivocal either, otherwise he could not produce his own likeness: so he can still be called an analogical agent;
- creatures' likeness to God is imperfect, because they do not represent the same thing even generically;
- God is not a measure that is in proportion to the things measured, so God and creatures do not need to be in the same genus.

Sixth Article   Whether Names Predicated of God Are Predicated Primarily of Creatures? (pp. 121–2)

The objections are:

- as creatures are known before God, the names used seem to be predicated primarily of creatures rather than of God;
- names transferred from creatures to God, such as 'lion' and 'stone', refer primarily to creatures, not God;
- names applied to both God and creatures apply to God as the cause of creatures, but what is applied to something's cause is applied to it secondarily.

Aquinas' answer is: when names are used analogically, they are predicated through a relation to one particular thing, which must be put in the definition of all of them. As the essence expressed by the name is the definition, the name must apply primarily to that which is put in the definition of the other things, and secondarily to the others, as they approximate to the first. Names applied metaphorically to God apply primarily to creatures, because they mean only similarities to such creatures. When the word 'lion' is applied to God, it means that God shows strength like a lion. With other names, the same would be the case only if they referred to God as cause. However, 'good' and 'wise' are applied to God, not just as cause, but essentially, signifying that the perfections exist in God more excellently, and apply primarily to him, because they flow from him to creatures. But, the names are applied primarily to creatures, as they are known first.

His replies to the objections are:

- the first is true to the extent that it applies to imposing the name;
- the same rule does not apply to metaphorical and other names;
- it would be valid only if the names applied to God as cause, not also essentially.

Twelfth Article   Whether Affirmative Propositions Can Be Formed About God? (pp. 132–4)

The objections are:

- it has been said that negations about God are true, but affirmations are vague;
- everything about which an affirmative proposition is made is a subject, but a simple form, like God, cannot be a subject;
- God has no composition, but to make an affirmation about something is to understand it as composite.

Aquinas' answer is: there are affirmative propositions of faith, such as that God is omnipotent, so they can be made about God. God is one and simple but, as we cannot see him as he is in himself, we know him by a number of ideas. However, we also know that only one reality corresponds to these ideas.

His replies to the objections are:

- what is affirmed of God is vague, because no name can be applied to God with exactly the same meaning as it has in ordinary usage;
- simple subsisting forms cannot be understood as they are in themselves, but only in the same way as composite things;
- human beings understand simple things in a composite way, but they do not think that they are composite things, so the intellect is not false in making a judgement about God.

Question XXV   The Power of God

Second Article   Whether the Power of God Is Infinite?
(pp. 260–2)

The objections are:

- God's power seems not to be infinite, for everything infinite is imperfect; but God's power is not;
- every power is known by its effect, so if God's power is infinite, it would produce an infinite effect, which is impossible;
- a corporeal thing with infinite power would cause movement instantaneously, but God does not, so he does not have infinite power.

Aquinas' answer is: God's being is infinite, so his active power should be infinite. The more perfectly an agent has the form by which it acts, the greater its power to act and, as the divine essence through which God acts is infinite, so is his power.

The replies to the objections are:

- an infinity belonging to matter is not limited by any form, but the divine essence is not like this, and so God's power is infinite and his power is not imperfect;
- a univocal agent's power is wholly shown in its effect, but God is not one, so his effect is always less than his power, so God's infinite power does not have to be shown in producing an infinite effect;
- a univocal agent's whole power would be shown in its motion, but not that of an incorporeal one.

Third Article   Whether God Is Omnipotent? (pp. 262–3)

The objections are:

- God does not have movement and passiveness, because he is immovable, so he is not omnipotent;
- sin is a kind of act, but is not possible for God, so he is not omnipotent;
- God is said to show his omnipotence particularly in having mercy, but there are greater acts;
- if God were omnipotent, everything would be possible and nothing impossible, but if the impossible is removed, the necessary is too, so if God were omnipotent, there would be nothing necessary, which is impossible.

Aquinas' answer is: God's omnipotence is universally acknowledged, but to say that God can do all things means all possible things, and there are two ways in which something is possible. The first is in relation to some power, like that of human beings, but God's omnipotence cannot relate to what is possible for creatures. God is omnipotent because he is able to do all things that are possible absolutely, but something involving being and non-being is not absolutely possible, and so cannot fall within God's omnipotence. This is not because his power is defective, but because it is not possible. Thus, God's omnipotence extends to everything that does not involve a contradiction in terms.

His replies to the objections are:

- God's omnipotence is in respect of active power, so is not incompatible with his immovability;
- God cannot sin, as to do so would be to fall short of the perfect;
- God's omnipotence is shown especially in having mercy, because he thus freely forgives sins, which is not the prerogative of an inferior power;
- with God, things are said to be possible in relation to a higher cause, and it is the proximate cause that determines whether the effect is contingent or necessary, but the world foolishly thinks that what is impossible for creatures is for God, too. However, God's omnipotence does not remove impossibility and necessity from things.

Fifth Article   Whether God Can Do what He Does not? (pp. 266–8)

The objections are:

- God cannot do what he has not foreknown and pre-ordained to do, so can only do what he does;
- he can only do what is just, and is not bound to do anything else;

- he cannot do anything to harm creation, and it would not be good for creatures to be other than they are.

Aquinas' answer is: some people mistakenly think that God acts from natural necessity, so that nothing can happen except what actually does. But God's will causes all things, so there is no necessity in the present scheme of things, ruling out things being otherwise. Others have argued that things must be as they are, due to God's wisdom and justice, but the wisdom with which he has established the order of creation is not restricted to it. The created order is not equal to God's wisdom, which could have produced a different one. God can do other things than those he has done.

His replies to the objections are:

- there is nothing in God's power that is not also found in his just will or wise intellect, so there is nothing to stop the divine power containing something that he does not will. By his absolute power, God could do different things from those he has foreknown and pre-ordained, but not do anything that he has not foreknown and pre-ordained;
- to say that God can do only what he ought means that he can only do what is just, but not that he is limited to the just things of the present order;
- creation is restricted to what now exists, but God's power and wisdom are not, so, while another order would not be suitable for things existing now, God could make other things and a different order.

Glossary

Absolute knowledge. Aquinas is responding to the argument that knowledge of God's existence is self-evident, because it exists naturally in human beings. However, as the knowledge of God, implanted by nature, is general and confused, it does not provide the absolute certainty of God's existence that Anselm had claimed in his *Proslogion*: that once the word 'God' is understood, it is seen that God must exist, as God is that than which nothing greater can be conceived, and actual existence is greater that mental existence, so it follows God must actually exist.

Absolute power. God's power is believed to be unlimited or infinite, so he is omnipotent.

Accident. A property of something which is not part of its essence, and which could be added to, or taken away from, it without it ceasing to be the same thing.

Active power. The power to act upon something else. God is active power in the highest degree.

Actuality/actually. That which is the case, as opposed to what could become so. Wood is potentially hot, but can only be made hot by something in a state of actuality: fire.

Affirmative proposition (about God). A statement that God positively is something, as opposed to ones that state what he is not. See affirmative proposition of faith below.

Glossary

Affirmative proposition of faith. A positive statement about God, which is based on revelation, not natural reason, such as that God is three and one (the Trinity).

Agent. One who performs an action.

Albert the Great, Saint (c. 1200–80). Dominican philosopher and theologian and Bishop of Ratisbon.

Analogous/analogical/analogy. In the *Summa Theologica*, using the similarities between God and creatures (which are known) as a basis for statements about God. This is possible, because there is a relation between God and creatures, that of cause and effect: creatures are God's effects. Such analogical statements about God are neither univocal nor equivocal. When it is said that God is 'good' or 'wise', it means that these perfections, which exist in creatures, exist in God in a more excellent way. Thus, the words apply primarily to God, as the perfections flow from him to his creatures, but their use begins with the creatures, who are known first.

Ancient philosophers. Philosophers of the ancient world, Greek philosophers.

Animate. Living.

Anselm, Saint (1033–1109). Italian-born philosopher and theologian, his writings include the *Monologion* and *Proslogion*. A Benedictine monk, Anselm became Abbot of the Norman Abbey of Bec in 1078, and succeeded Lanfranc as Archbishop of Canterbury in 1093.

Antecedent. Previous, what comes before.

A posteriori. That which comes after, or is based on, experience/empirical evidence.

A priori. That which comes before experience, and which holds (or is claimed to hold) irrespective of experience.

Aristotle (384–322 BC). Greek philosopher and student of Plato.

Author of such books as *De Interpretatione, Nicomachean Ethics* and *Metaphysics*. His philosophical ideas (Aristotelianism) had an enormous influence on medieval thinkers, such as Thomas Aquinas, who refers to him as 'The Philosopher'.

Article of faith. Religious belief/principle that is held on the basis of faith, and which may conflict with empirical evidence.

Augustine, Saint (354–430). Christian philosopher and theologian, and Bishop of Hippo in North Africa. Author of *Confessions* and *The City of God*.

Beatitude. Perfect happiness/blessedness, which human beings can only achieve after death when they see God's essence.

Body. God does not have a body. A body only moves if it is moved, but God is the first mover, and is himself unmoved. As the first being, he must, unlike a body, be in act, not potentiality.

Boethius, Anicus Manilus Severinus (c. 480–524). Roman philosopher and consul. Author of *De Consolatione Philosophae*.

Canonization. Recognition by the Roman Catholic Church of a person as a saint.

Cause. That which brings about a certain effect, as in God being the cause of the universe.

Changeable things. Unlike God, created things change: they come into existence and they cease to exist.

Chrysostom, St John (c. 347–407). Christian theologian, Archbishop of Constantinople and author of commentaries on the Bible.

Composite. Something made up of parts.

Conceive. Think of.

Conditional proposition. A proposition the truth of which depends on another proposition, such as, 'If God made the world, we can obtain knowledge about him from the world.'

Consequent. Resulting, that which follows,

Contingency (of existence/effect). That which could not-be, or which might not have occurred and depends on something else for its existence/occurrence. See also necessity and something that has necessary existence below.

Contradiction. When a proposition and its negation are brought together. Aquinas explains (Quest. XXV, Art. 3) that when it is said that God is able to do all things, this means all things that are absolutely possible, not those involving a contradiction in terms.

Copleston, Frederick Charles (1907–94). Philosopher and Jesuit priest, whose books include *Aquinas* and the multi-volume *A History of Philosophy*.

Corporeal parts. Bodily parts.

Corrupted. Perishing, deteriorating: a feature of all things found in nature.

Cosmological argument. One of the traditional arguments for the existence of God, which argues from God's effects (the world) to his existence. This is the kind of argument Aquinas puts forward in his five ways (Quest. II, Art. 3). Although still widely accepted, the cosmological argument was rejected by David Hume in Part IX of his *Dialogues Concerning Natural Religion* (see Context) and Immanuel Kant in Book II, Chapter III, Section V of his *Critique of Pure Reason*.

Created intellect. The mind of a created being, such as a human being.

Creation. The idea that the universe was made by God (from nothing, according to Christian teaching), rather than coming into existence as the result of natural processes.

Creator. Term applied to God as the maker of the universe.

Creature. Something created including, if God made the world, human beings.

Defect(s). The faults or shortcomings found in the world, which consists of changeable things.

Demonstrate. Prove something conclusively.

Denominated. Given a name by, identified by.

Designedly. In a way that shows design, as a result of being directed by God. In his fifth way, Aquinas maintains that even natural bodies act for an end, to obtain the best result, and so must be directed towards their end by some intelligent being: God.

Determinate end. Limited, finite. Nature works for a determinate end under God's direction.

Dionysius, the Areopagite. Paul converted him to Christianity (see Acts 17.34), and he is believed to have been Bishop of Athens. Such books as *On the Heavenly and Ecclesiastical Names*, *On Divine Names* and *On Mystical Theology* used to be attributed to him, but it is now thought they were written centuries later.

Divine nature. God's nature.

Divine substance. God's essence.

Doctrine. (Religious) dogma or belief.

Dominion. Sovereignty or control.

Effect(s). What results from an action. In the *Summa Theologica*, specifically the created world/creatures, which are a source of our knowledge of God, and enable us to establish his existence through the use of natural reason.

Efficient cause. The cause that produces the particular effect, and which makes a thing what it is.

Empirical. That which relates to, or is based on, experience.

Equivocal. When a term is used in relation to two things and has a completely different meaning.

Equivocal cause/agent. God is an equivocal cause, and so, although his effects bear a likeness to him, he greatly exceeds them.

Essence. The essential nature of something, that which makes something what it is, and without which it would not be what it is.

Eternal/eternity. In the Christian context, the idea that God transcends time. There is no past, present or future in God, who endures beyond every kind of given duration.

Evil. That which is opposed to good and to God.

Existence of God. Quest. II is concerned with God's existence and whether it can be proved by natural reason. According to Aquinas, there are five ways in which God's existence can be proved (Quest. II, Art. 3).

Faith. In a religious context, this can be simply religious belief/belief in God, or trusting belief in God (his existence and/or his goodness), which is not supported by clear evidence.

Finite. Limited.

First being. God.

First cause. God. In the second of the five ways, Aquinas argues that, as everything has a cause, there must either be an infinite regress of causes or a first cause and, as there cannot be an infinite regress of causes, there must be a first cause of the world: God.

First mover. God. In the first of the five ways, Aquinas argues that there are things in the world that are in motion, and what moves is moved by something else, as nothing can move itself. But this cannot go on to infinity, otherwise there would be no first, or any other, mover. So, there must be a first mover, moved by no other: God.

First principle. God.

Five ways. The five proofs of God's existence that Aquinas puts forward in the *Summa Theologica* (Quest. II, Art. 3), which argue from our experience of the world to God's existence.

Foreknow. To know beforehand. God knows everything beforehand, because he is omniscient.

Form(s). As Aquinas explains (Quest. VI, Art. 4), Plato argued that the essences of things exist separately, as transcendent forms, which cause, and gave identity to, individual things in the world, which approximate to them. Thus, Socrates was a man through participation in the form of a man.

Generated. To have been brought into existence, as changeable natural things have.

Genus. Class of things, which have common characteristics, but which can be divided into different species.

God. In the *Summa Theologica*, the Christian God.

Governance of the world. How the world operates, as determined by God.

Grace. The help God freely gives to human beings through Jesus Christ; the means of understanding and accepting in faith what God has revealed of himself to human beings.

Gradation of things. The extent to which things are more or less good. In his fourth way, Aquinas argues that things are more or less good to the extent that they resemble a maximum, which causes their goodness (God), as fire, the maximum of heat, causes all hot things.

Higher agent. God.

Holy scripture. The Bible.

Homogeneous. Of the same kind.

Human reason. Human beings' ability to reason. Human

reason can establish certain truths about God, such as his existence, but revelation is needed for those truths about God that are beyond human reason. Aquinas makes the point that the truths, discoverable by reason, are available only to a few (those capable of following philosophical arguments).

Hume, David (1711–76). Scottish empiricist philosopher and historian, whose works include the *Treatise of Human Nature, An Enquiry Concerning Human Understanding* and the *Dialogues Concerning Natural Religion.*

Image. According to Genesis 1.26, human beings are made in the image or likeness of God.

Immaterial substances. Non-physical beings.

Immovable. That which cannot be moved. God is immovable.

Immutable. Unchangeable. God is immutable.

Implanted in us by nature. See absolute knowledge above.

Inanimate. Not living.

Incorporeal. Not bodily, not composed of matter.

Inferior power. Lesser power. A lesser power than God would not be able to forgive sins (Quest. XXV, Art. 3).

Infinite. Unlimited.

Infinite goodness. God's goodness is believed to be unlimited, so he is all-good or omnibenevolent.

Infusion of divine light. Aquinas argues that human beings' ability to understand the natural images, received from the senses, is assisted by divine light (Quest. XII, Art. 13).

Intellect. Mind, faculty of knowing and understanding.

Intellect's natural light. The human mind's natural abilities.

Intelligent being. God, who directs natural bodies, which lack knowledge, towards their end, as an archer does an arrow.

Intelligible concepts. Comprehensible ideas, ideas that can be understood.

Intermediate cause(s). Causes that come between the first cause and the ultimate or final cause that produces an effect. In the second way, Aquinas argues that it does not matter how many intermediate causes there are; without a first cause, there would be no other causes, and thus no effects (Quest. II, Art. 3).

Invisible things of God. The unseen things of God. Aquinas is referring to Romans 1.20, in which Paul states that the invisible things of God, his eternal power and divine nature, can be known from what he has made: his effects, the world (Quest. II, Art. 2)

Jesus Christ. (c. BC 5/6–c. 30 AD). Founder of Christianity, who is the incarnate Word of God and second person of the Trinity.

Just/justice. Treating people fairly, people being treated fairly or receiving their due. In the *Summa Theologica*, there are references both to God's justice and to those who behave justly.

Local terminus. A physical destination. Aquinas (Quest. III, Art. 1) is discussing the dangers of being misled by biblical passages which refer to God in physical terms.

Material creatures. Created beings with bodies, such as human beings.

Material things. Things in the material world, physical things.

Matter. That from which physical things are made. The ancient philosophers classified matter into earth, air, fire and water, which were the different forms of primary or prime matter.

Maximum. The highest possible level or quantity. See gradation of things above.

Mentally. In the mind. Aquinas (Quest. II, Art. 1) is referring to Anselm's argument that actual existence is greater than mental existence. See also Anselm above and ontological argument below.

Mercy. God's omnipotence is shown especially in his mercy, as he freely forgives the sins of human beings.

Metaphorically/metaphor. Figure of speech that applies names or descriptions to objects in a non-literal way, in order to draw attention to, emphasize or make clear some point about them.

Metaphysics. What is after (beyond) physics, and which cannot be investigated by ordinary empirical methods; the investigation of what really exists, of ultimate reality.

Middle term. The middle term of a syllogism.

Mover and moved. See first mover above.

Natural body(ies). Physical objects without intellectual powers.

Natural knowledge. Knowledge obtained from the material world through experience, empirical knowledge.

Natural reason. Human beings' ability to reason and to acquire knowledge through experience. Aquinas believed that God's existence, for example, can be established by natural reason (Quest. II, Art. 3).

Natural theology. What human beings can find out about God through the use of their reason and from experience, without the help of revelation.

Necessary existence. See something that has necessary existence below.

Necessity (of existence/effect). That which is not something that could not-be, something which must occur/have occurred. See also contingency above and something that has necessary existence below.

Non-being. That which is opposed to being. Something that involves being and non-being, such as somebody being a man and an ass at the same time, is not absolutely possible, and so does not come within the scope of God's powers, because it involves a contradiction in terms, (Quest. XXV, Art. 3).

Omnipotence. God is believed to be infinitely powerful or omnipotent.

Ontological argument. One of the traditional arguments for the existence of God, put forward by St Anselm in his *Proslogion*, which argues from the concept of God to his existence. See Detailed Summary (Quest. II, Art. 1) and Context.

Pagan. One who worships a false god(s), and (in the context of the *Summa Theologica*) who is not a Christian.

Participation. Taking part in. Things that are good participate in God's goodness (Quest. VI, Art. 4).

Paul, Saint (believed to have died 64–8 AD). Christian missionary and theologian, who, after his conversion to Christianity, dedicated his life to preaching Christianity to the Gentiles (non-Jews). Paul's letters or epistles to the Christian churches form part of the New Testament.

Perfect knowledge. Complete knowledge.

Perfection. Either perfect quality or being perfected, made perfect.

Philosophical disciplines. The range of academic disciplines which, in medieval times, were grouped under philosophy, thus including the various branches of science.

Philosophy. Literally, love of wisdom. The study of ultimate reality, what really exists, the most general principles of things.

Plato (c. 429–347 BC). Greek philosopher, whose writings include *The Republic, Theaetetus, Symposium, Phaedrus* and *Laws*. See also form(s) above.

Possibility and necessity. See something that has necessary existence below.

Potentiality. What could become the case. Wood has the potential to be hot, and becomes actually so when fire (which is in a state of actuality) is applied to it.

Preamble. What is preparatory to something else, as, according to Aquinas, natural knowledge is to faith.

Predicate. The part of a statement/proposition in which something is said about the subject. In the statement, 'Socrates is a philosopher', 'is a philosopher' is the predicate.

Pre-exist. Exist before.

Pre-ordain. Decide, order beforehand.

Present scheme of things. The way that creation, the world, is ordered at the moment. God (Quest. XXV, Art. 5) has established the present order, but he was not bound by any necessity to make it as it is, so it was within his power to have established a different order of creation.

Primal truth. A major religious truth, such as God's existence.

Prior to itself. Before itself. For something to be the cause of itself, it would have to exist before itself, which would be impossible (Quest. II, Art. 3).

Problem of evil. The problem that arises from the apparent contradiction between the presence of evil in the world and the belief that it was created by an omnipotent and good God.

Procession. Movement from, out of.

Proof. Showing that something is true.

Proposition. Statement, which may or may not be true.

Proximate cause. Nearest, immediate cause.

Pure act. God is pure act as he has no potentiality (Quest. IX, Art. 1).

Rational creatures. Creatures with reason, human beings.

Reveal(ed)/revelation. What God chooses to disclose of himself to human beings through, for example, prophets and holy scriptures.

Revealed theology. What we can find out/know about God from revelation. See also natural theology.

Russell, Bertrand Arthur William, third Earl Russell (1872–1970). Cambridge philosopher and mathematician, Nobel prize winner and peace campaigner, whose books include *Principia Mathematica*, *The Problems of Philosophy* and the *History of Western Philosophy*.

Sacred doctrine. The religious truths that God has made known to human beings through revelation.

Salvation. Human beings being saved from sin and death through God having made known religious truths to them through revelation (Quest. I, Art. 1).

Scientific knowledge. Knowledge that has been established by ordinary empirical methods, as opposed to knowledge that comes from revelation, which has to be accepted in faith.

Scripture. The Bible, which is held to be inspired by God.

Self-evident. Completely obvious, as is the truth of a proposition in which the predicate is included in the definition of the subject.

Self-evident proposition. A proposition in which the predicate is included in the essence or definition of the subject, as in 'man is an animal' (Quest. II, Art. 1).

Self-necessary first principle. See something that has necessary existence below.

Self-subsisting. Does not depend upon anything else for its existence/continuing existence.

Sensible things. Things which can be known through the senses.

Signification. What a word signifies or means.

Similitude. Resemblance (to).

Simple/simplicity. Not consisting of parts, not composite.

Simple subsistents. Things that are simple, in that they are not composite.

Socrates (c. 470–399 BC). Greek philosopher, who features in the works of Plato, and devoted his life to the pursuit of philosophical truth. He was executed by the Athenian authorities for undermining belief in the gods and corrupting youth.

Soul. In Christianity, the spiritual element within human beings, which is the seat of personality and individual identity, which lives on after death, and which will be reunited with its body at the general resurrection.

Something that has necessary existence. In his third way or proof of God's existence, Aquinas argues from the world, which contains generated and corrupted things that can not-be, to something that has necessary existence: God. See Detailed Summary (Quest. II, Art. 3) and Context.

Species. The subgroups into which a genus is divided.

Spirit. Being that does not have a body.

Spiritual being. See spirit above.

Subject. The word or words in a statement/proposition about which something is predicated.

Substance. The essence of something, which makes it what it is.

Superexceed. Infinitely surpass, as God does his creatures.

Suppositum. The subject of a statement or proposition.

Syllogism. A form of reasoning, in which, from two propositions or premises with a common or middle term, a third can be inferred, from which the common term is absent.

Teleological argument. Argument from the apparently purposeful behaviour of even non-rational and inanimate things in the world to an intelligent being who directs them towards their end.

Temporal things. Things that are of this world and therefore subject to the laws of time (and space). Aquinas points out that, because their experience is limited to the empirical world, human beings can only understand the concept of eternity through temporal things, as these are the things to which their intellects relate (Quest. XIII, Art. 1).

That than which nothing greater can be conceived. See ontological argument above.

Theology. Generally: setting out the beliefs and teachings of a religion in a systematic way; academic discipline concerned with the study of religion/religious beliefs and teachings. Aquinas distinguishes between natural theology and theology based on revelation (Quest. I, Art. 1).

Thomist. Admirer or follower of Thomas Aquinas' philosophical and theological ideas.

Three and One. In Christianity, God exists in three, co-equal persons: Father, Son and Holy Spirit (the Trinity). However, this does not mean that God is divided into three or there are three Gods. God's unity is preserved, because the three persons are of one substance (of one being) and so God is three in one. The teaching has been a subject of debate and (intense) disagreement over the centuries. It is helpful to think in terms of three modes of existence: God the Father: the creator; God the Son: Jesus, the redeemer; and the Holy Spirit: the inspirer and sustainer of Christians and the Christian Church.

Transcendence. Being above or apart from the material or empirical world, as God is.

Ultimate cause. The immediate cause of the effect.

Ultimate perfection. The final making perfect of human beings will occur when they achieve beatitude, and see God's essence (Quest. XII, Art. 1).

Unity. Oneness. God is perfect oneness, one reality, but, because of the limitations of their experience and understanding, human beings find this difficult to grasp (Quest. XIII, Art. 4).

Univocal. When a word is used in relation to two things and has exactly the same meaning.

Univocal agent/cause. God is not a univocal agent or cause, because he is completely different from his effects and, therefore, his effects fall short of him.

Vision of comprehension. Vision of God, when human beings will see God's essence.

Voluntary things. Things that happen as a result of human decisions, by voluntary acts of the human will.

The Briefly Series

Briefly: Anselm's *Proslogion*

Briefly: Aquinas' *Summa Theologica I*

Briefly: Aquinas' *Summa Theologica II*

Briefly: Descartes' *Meditation on the First Philosophy*

Briefly: Hume's *Dialogues Concerning Natural Religion*

Briefly: Kant's *Groundwork of the Metaphysics of Morals*

Briefly: Mill's *Utilitarianism*

Briefly: Mill's *On Liberty*

Briefly: Plato's *The Republic*